CHAOTIC
EATING

by Helen Bray-Garretson, Ph.D.
and Kaye V. Cook, Ph.D.

ZondervanPublishingHouse
Grand Rapids, Michigan

A Division of HarperCollins*Publishers*

Chaotic Eating
Copyright © 1992 by Helen Bray-Garretson and Kaye V. Cook

Requests for information should be addressed to:
Zondervan Publishing House
Grand Rapids, Michigan 49530

Library of Congress Cataloging-in-Publication Data

Bray-Garretson, Helen.
    Chaotic eating / by Helen Bray-Garretson and Kaye V. Cook.
      p. cm.
    Includes bibliographical references.
    ISBN 0-310-57401-3
    1. Eating disorders—Patients—Religious life. 2. Eating
disorders—Religious aspects—Christianity. I. Cook, Kaye V.
II. Title.
BV4910.4.B73   1992
362.1'968526—dc20   91–43962
                                                CIP

Edited by Betsey Newenhuyse
Interior designed by Ann Cherryman
Cover designed by The Church Art Works

Printed in the United States of America

92 93 94 95 96 / ML / 10 9 8 7 6 5 4 3 2 1

Contents

We dedicate this book to our daughters,
Eleanor, Jenni, and Julia,
in the hope that
they will always be free to eat
in a spiritually, physically, and
emotionally healthy way.

1. *Every Woman's Obsession*

I think about food more than I think about God. In the morning when I get up, it's with me: I'm wondering what and how much I am going to eat today. I even daydream in church about the different tastes and textures that are in those fancy candies, like truffles and Almond Roca. But when I eat, I refuse food that looks good and choose something that looks healthy, something with few calories. The only time I really enjoy food is when my mind is totally turned off and I let my mouth take over. It scares me to be so obsessed by eating.

—Linda, age twenty-six

Many of us can identify with Linda, whether we're twenty-six or fifty-six. We're obsessed with eating, or not eating. We fear food; we love food; we start diets; we blow diets. When we're teenagers we compare our bodies to magazine models or rock stars or other girls in gym class, and invariably we can find something to hate. We go to college and gain weight and are filled with self-loathing. We get married, have babies, and fret about shedding postpregnancy pounds. We lunch with coworkers and order "just a salad, dressing on the side," then we go home, exhausted, and secretly treat ourselves to ice cream out of the carton.

Christian women are just as likely as other women to fall victim to confused, inappropriate, chaotic attitudes toward food. Food preoccupies our thought life. We may feel that food controls us. We fear food, rather than appreciate it as a good gift from God. Our bodies feel like fat blobs to be thwarted and thinned rather than temples to be built up and nurtured for the indwelling presence of God.

Many Christians experience a deeply rooted ambivalence about the meaning of food in their lives. In a survey of young women at an evangelical Christian college, sixty-seven percent of the women agreed that they gave too much time and thought to eating, seventy-four percent were scared of being overweight, and sixty-seven percent admitted that they felt guilty after eating anything at all. Only four percent were not concerned about their eating habits.[1] Christian women are overly concerned about their eating because they fear that their body is or may become too fat.

Are You a Chaotic Eater?

Many for whom this book is written may not admit that eating is a problem. Yet you spend so much time worrying about food, your weight, and feeding others that you deplete the energy that should be devoted to pursuing God's highest and best calling in your lives. You may have an eating problem if

- ☐ you evaluate whether you are thinner or fatter than everyone you meet.
- ☐ you feel guilty about every calorie you eat.
- ☐ you pray daily about eating.
- ☐ you eat in secret.
- ☐ you buy clothes a size too small to inspire you to lose weight.
- ☐ you watch carefully what other people eat.
- ☐ you binge.
- ☐ your closet has unused or briefly used weight reducing or exercise gimmicks in it.
- ☐ you've considered making yourself vomit or taking laxatives after you've eaten too much.
- ☐ you are constantly on a diet.

☐ you try to skip breakfast or lunch.
☐ you eat without tasting your food.
☐ you think God loves you more when you are thin.

Eating problems are marked by obsessions with food that lead to unhealthy eating patterns. We will address three specific forms of chaotic eating: compulsive eating and dieting, bulimia, and anorexia nervosa. However, it is not unusual to find eating problems that resemble these but are less extreme or that swing from one to another of these categories.

Maria describes her eating as "out of control" since she was twelve. She has been on a diet "constantly" since then. She finds that she generally gains weight during the winter and loses weight in the spring just in time for trying on new bathing suits. Maria works in a deli and, while at work, forces herself to nibble from the green salads, although she can't help imagining what the pesto tastes like. Every now and then, she attacks the pesto, eating so much that her boss docks her pay. Maria is a compulsive eater.

Maria fits into the largest category of chaotic eaters, those women who are relentless dieters and compulsive eaters. They may be of average weight, or excessively thin or heavy. Their friends may not be aware of their struggles with food, yet they themselves feel frightened and overwhelmed by the feelings that drive them to eat and to diet. This cycle between episodic overeating and compulsive dieting is so common in our culture that most of us assume it is normal, even healthy. But in fact repetitive undereating and overeating, repetitively losing and gaining weight, jeopardizes our health and undermines our self-esteem.

Janet eats well much of the time. But tonight she "lost it" and realizes too late that she has just eaten a half gallon of ice cream and a whole package of Fig Newtons. She is furious at her binge and makes herself vomit in the

bathroom while she runs the water full blast. She remem-
bers then that she had felt stressed out. After all, the
pressure was on her at work and, to make it worse, she had
no plans for the weekend. But why did she have to eat so
much?

Janet is a bulimic eater. *Bulimics* are dieters who periodically break out into food binges, overeating compulsively.
When they realize what they have done, they panic and
attempt to purge away the calories they have ingested. They
may begin an extreme diet, exercise obsessively, use laxatives
or induce vomiting. Bulimics generally feel anxious and depressed about their chaotic eating and try to keep their binges a
secret from others. They feel powerless to escape the diet-
binge-purge cycle.

Delia weighs eighty-six pounds, counts calories in every-
thing she eats, and does aerobic workouts for two hours
every day. Despite her parents' concern, she is delighted at
the forty pounds she has lost this past year. She feels that
she finally has control over her body.

Anorexia nervosa is the most dramatic eating disorder, and
the least common. An anorexic is a compulsive dieter who eats
so little and so abnormally that her body weight is markedly
below normal, yet she perceives herself as "fat." As in Delia's
case, she generally disregards the opinions of others and may
congratulate herself on her self-control. She does not recognize
that her eating patterns are self-destructive. An anorexic may
deny for years that she needs treatment, even though her
health, even her life, may be in danger.

You do *not* necessarily have a problem if you think you
"look fat." An eating problem is marked by chaotic eating
patterns and distorted ideas about food rather than by one's
feelings about one's weight or looks. The borderlines between
obesity, overweight, and "just right" are subjective and poorly
defined. Many people who feel overweight are in fact at a

reasonable weight for their body frame and metabolism—even if they are not rail-thin. We should use facts about our eating rather than our too quickly assumed sense of "feeling fat" as evidence of an eating problem.

For Women Only?

Eating problems are primarily women's problems. Approximately ninety-five percent of bulimics and anorexics are women. In our survey of students at a Christian college, eighty percent of the men expressed minimal concern about eating while seventy percent of the women expressed moderate to extreme concern.[2] While many men may have unhealthy patterns of eating, they seem to experience less distress about it, probably because society does not hold such rigid standards about thinness for men as for women. Men can compensate in other ways such as achievement, making money, athletic prowess, or being articulate in public. A woman may be a high achiever in the business world or other arena, but if her body does not measure up to some mythical, self-imposed standard, she will probably struggle with self-esteem. In this book, we will speak primarily to and of women, but the principles of healthy eating and the specific strategies for dealing appropriately with food apply equally well to men.

Getting Our Eating and Moving in Balance

We should be concerned with *how we eat* and *how we move* rather than *how we look*. We have little choice about the basic shape of our bodies, but we have a great deal of choice about how we eat and live. Humans, created in the image of God, come in all sizes and shapes: paunchy, scrawny, rotund, muscular, flabby, saggy, thin, or fat. God has created us uniquely, and wants us to appreciate the beauty in our diversity.

While the Bible includes lessons about eating socially to build community and to observe a sacrament, the major purpose of eating is to satisfy physical hunger, and in so doing provide nourishment. God wants us to eat in a way that satisfies our hunger and strengthens our bodies without abusing food.

Over the past 100 years the American lifestyle has become increasingly sedentary. We are becoming a nation of couch potatoes. When I ask families during a counseling session what they do together as a family, the most usual response is "We watch television together." Sitting passively, without interacting, sharing a laugh about a ridiculous sitcom may be relaxing, but it may also be a form of psychological paralysis. What has happened to physically vigorous, mentally active, emotionally engaging family activities?

We depend on so many labor-saving devices in the household that even homemaking does not offer as much energy output for us as it used to. Why mix by hand when we can use a food processor? Why bother to hang clothes on a clothesline when we can push a button to dry our clothes? Why rake leaves when we can vacuum them? Our conveniences have robbed us of our chance to integrate physical movement into our daily activities.

Our eating experience is often disconnected from our energy output. We should eat in order to strengthen our bodies for service—for actively doing something. Too often, however, we protect ourselves from energy expenditure. For the person who wants to overcome chaotic eating, activity is a necessary part of the formula for trusting and loving one's body. This means that some women will choose an exercise program, a commitment to physical movement in a disciplined, repetitive way. For others this may mean consciously integrating physical movement back into their life by using stairs instead of elevators or parking in the farthest parking spot rather than circling the lot hunting for the closest. Movement puts you more in touch with your body, more sensitive to its changes, and more aware of how eating affects your body.

Where then is the sin in eating? It is not necessarily in being overweight, or in enjoying our food, or in going off our diet. Dieting is not evidence of our obedience to God, and thinness is not next to godliness. The goal of eating is to provide energy for our body's work. The sin is in letting our eating dominate our lives and the quest for personal beauty take precedence over spiritual growth. We eat to nurture ourselves when we eat to satisfy hunger, strengthen our bodies, and mobilize our energy for service to God.

Why Is It So Hard?

You can quit drinking or smoking, but you cannot quit eating. It is an issue every day for every person. Further confusing the issue are the cultural, personal, and spiritual dynamics that can make such a simple act as deciding what to have for dinner a complicated decision indeed!

The cultural dynamic. Attitudes toward eating in contemporary American society are distorted, and it may be that all Americans experience eating problems. Our culture overvalues thinness; we admire people who have the willpower to avoid eating. Yet typically we eat unhealthy food on irregular schedules, or indulge ourselves with food that has little nutritional value. Americans value variety in food, rushing to try the latest sugar cereal, the fanciest brand name, or the newest restaurant. We relish the ready availability of fast foods, gourmet items, and low-calorie food to zap in the microwave. Many families rarely eat together other than snack foods in front of the television. Women's magazines tout the latest diet on one page and show mouth-watering spreads of chocolate desserts on the next. No wonder we're confused.

Most Christians assume that God wants women to be as thin as the fashion models in *Vogue* magazine. And not just *Vogue*—Christian periodicals, too, tend to feature stereotypically thin, beautiful women, giving the impression that slimness is somehow connected to spirituality. Even when we know we cannot be as thin as the latest model, we still envy her.

The personal dynamic. Eating patterns are rooted in early emotional experiences of food. Parents may feed children to quiet them whenever they are crying from anger or hurt. Children may learn that food fills the emptiness inside caused by loneliness or depression. Eating may begin to dull and camouflage emotional pain of all sorts: anger, anxiety, boredom, frustration, confusion, and guilt. Our emotional histories complicate eating, making unhealthy patterns harder to correct.

Eating becomes confused with identity and self-esteem issues and substitutes for satisfaction of our deepest needs. Food is no longer just food; it transforms into the enemy, the cause of self-rejection, the source of relationship problems. When the binge occurs—as it always will—women experience it as personal failure, and their self-esteem goes down a notch. Many adult women never grow out of this mindset. One woman commented, "I know I can't do anything right in my life because I can't even make myself thin."

The spiritual dynamic. Many Christian women are so absorbed in their struggle with food and in judging their eating as sinful that they miss more important issues in their spiritual lives. Repeated failures at dieting erode a woman's self-confidence and ability to take on personal, spiritual, and emotional challenges in other areas of life. Eating is not an incidental characteristic of our lives, divorced from our Christianity and of no interest to God. Eating is one manifestation of our lives as Christians. Wrong eating can produce spiritual chaos, numbness, faith conflicts, and alienation from God. When our minds and our mouths are consumed with our eating problems, God is pushed to the periphery of our souls.

The symbolism of eating appears in the first chapter of Genesis and pervades the Old and New Testaments, partly because it is a universally shared experience. Eating is a powerful expression of our personal needs and our ability to trust in one another. Remember the stories about God feeding the Israelites in times of famine, the rules about food consumption in the Law, the miraculous ways God fed the prophets, and the lessons Jesus taught with food and eating? Eating is constantly mentioned, often as an everyday act with profound significance, like the widow cooking for Elijah, Jesus eating with Zacchaeus, and Joseph's brothers coming to Egypt for food. Biblical references to hunger and food illustrate spiritual issues and principles but also can offer us practical advice about the place of eating in our lives.

The Bible uses eating to symbolize both sin and redemption. Eve ate the forbidden fruit, and humankind willfully separated themselves from God. Yet in the New Testament, Jesus asks us to remember him through a ritual of eating: breaking the bread and sharing the cup. God's promises to us are often described in terms of food: the Promised Land flowing with milk and honey, the table prepared for us in the presence of our enemies, the heavenly marriage feast. Our sinfulness, our redemption, and our ultimate restoration become real to us as we understand our own eating. By its intensity and universality, eating becomes a pivotal experience of faith, yet an experience that is often ignored because it seems so mundane.

Self-Help or Professional Help?

If you are struggling with an eating problem, should you seek help or try to solve the problem yourself? We generally recommend professional intervention for all eating concerns. First, professional intervention is critical for anorexics and bulimics, beginning as early as possible. Both are potentially life-threatening. Compulsive eating and dieting, although less immediately life-threatening, can lead to depression and low self-esteem. Obsessive focus on food can keep us from experiencing the rich, full life we have been promised as Christians. Professional help can help to break the destructive thought patterns that lead to chaotic eating. You should seek professional help from a counselor when

- ☐ you feel chronically depressed about eating patterns.
- ☐ you feel lethargic, groggy, and faint for lack of eating.
- ☐ you develop headaches or back pains, or some other physical symptom, possibly associated with eating.

- [ ] concerns about eating consume a large part of your thought life.
- [ ] you feel helpless enough to consider suicide.
- [ ] you are rapidly losing weight.
- [ ] you have lost fifteen percent of your body weight within a relatively short period of time.
- [ ] you stop menstruating.
- [ ] you use diuretics or laxatives to purge.
- [ ] you induce vomiting on a regular basis.
- [ ] eating problems persist over several years.

Personally, we have seen the chaotic-eating problem from many perspectives. As psychologists and as counselors on Christian college campuses we have listened to hundreds of women tell their stories about eating. We have counseled women with eating problems ranging from those mildly anxious about overeating to those dealing with life-threatening anorexia and bulimia. We are both daughters in food-focused families, and we are mothers of daughters who seem like finicky eaters until we recall that children are more in touch with their real physical hunger than we are. We understand the way that chaotic eating can dominate a woman's life, and we believe that every person can overcome their bondage to food.

In this book, we outline principles that can be applied personally or, with some revisions, by professionals. We do not believe that serious eating problems are generally amenable to self-treatment. But we do believe that all Christians, whether eating-disordered or not, whether in treatment or not, need to understand the centrality of eating in spiritual life—and how we can approach food in a balanced way, not fearing it, not hating it. We believe it is possible to make friends with food—to eat as God intended.

Remolding Our Minds from Within

There are no easy answers to any eating problem. As we will discuss in the following chapters, eating problems require complex, long-term solutions. The apostle Paul distinguishes between Christian thought and action, a distinction that is also helpful in understanding eating. Change must occur in a person's attitudes toward food *and* in one's eating behaviors. One must give up the unrelenting pursuit of thinness, developing a more realistic self-assessment. One must also identify and change the specific situations, foods, and feelings that trigger wrong eating.

Our theme is best summarized in Romans 12:1–2, here modified from the Phillips translation:

> *With eyes wide open to the mercies of God, I beg you, my brothers and sisters, as an act of intelligent worship, to give God your bodies, as a living sacrifice, consecrated to God and acceptable by God. Don't let the world around you squeeze you into its mold, but let God remold your minds from within, so that you may prove in practice that God's plan for you is good, meeting all tests and demands and moving you towards the goal of true maturity.*

Give God your bodies as a living sacrifice. Recognize that God accepts you and your body no matter what its condition. While God may not care about your body size, God does care about your eating attitudes and choices about physical activity. Eating is not to be trivialized nor is it to be an overpowering force that dominates our spiritual lives and our self-esteem. Nor is body movement to be shameful, ignored, or on the other hand, overemphasized. With God's help we can learn to eat and exercise appropriately.

Don't let the world squeeze you into its mold. We should struggle to reflect the image of God, not the image of a fashion plate or movie star. We do not need to read all the recipes, try all the diets, or buy all the exercise gimmicks that are advertised in the women's magazines. God offers a higher calling: seek to serve God and show love to a needy world. We need to proclaim Christian values loudly and clearly rather than accepting the world's standards of beauty.

Let God remake your minds from within. Learn to trust your body's needs for eating and physical movement. Stop dieting, as it substitutes external standards for internal and is often ineffective. Replace the inflexibility of dieting and exercise programs with more reasonable guidelines generated from an awareness of your personal, physical hunger and your body's need for activity.

Move toward the goal of true maturity. Eating should not substitute for confronting emotional pain, dealing with relationship difficulties, or overcoming spiritual emptiness. Deal directly with these hungers without confusing them with physical hunger. The ideal is to be responsive to God, following the forward movement of God's leading in your life. What is God calling you to be, to do, to become? Confront your fears of change, leave eating problems behind, and move on to effective spiritual action that builds you up as you in turn sustain others.

Struggling toward this goal can make us stronger and more effective Christians. Breaking our bondage to food opens us up to becoming more authentically ourselves and more wholeheartedly God's. Self-nurturant eating, eating to take care of ourselves, is possible, even for chaotic eaters, bulimics, and anorexics. It is our prayer that Christians who have experienced healing at the Lord's Table can experience healing at their own daily table.

2.

Can Fat Hurt You?

I started gaining weight when I was nineteen. I had just married and quickly gotten pregnant. I was delighted to be pregnant but felt so isolated. Soon after my marriage, I felt my husband wasn't very warm or supportive, so I focused all my energies on my body and my baby. Now it's twenty years later, my weight is twice what it was then, and I've been fat as long as I was skinny. I can't remember when I wasn't on a diet.

—Jackie, age thirty-nine

"I have to admit it," said Lydia, who is in her early fifties. "When I see someone who's really overweight—as opposed to 'just needs to lose a few pounds'—I feel a certain contempt. I think I'm probably more judgmental because I've lost a lot of weight over the past few years. But I know it's not a very Christian way to think."

What do you think when you see someone whom you consider overweight? That she's sloppy, undisciplined, putting her health and longevity at risk? Do you think, *Thank God I'm not her?*

We diet to avoid becoming fat. Yet is fat such a villain? Myths about obesity are so strongly embedded in our culture that many of us fear fat more than almost anything else. The following exercise is meant to help you become aware of your own attitudes toward weight.

Exercise:
What Does
Weight
Mean to
You?

1. Close your eyes, lean back in your chair, and imagine yourself at a party. What are you doing? Are you sitting quietly by yourself, watching others? Are you in the middle of a group of people? What makes you feel safe in a crowd?
2. Imagine that you have gained fifteen pounds and are at the same party. What are you doing now? How have your feelings changed? Why? Do you feel safer? What do you fear?
3. Imagine that you have lost fifteen pounds. Now how do you feel?[1]

Myths About Obesity

Obesity is of tremendous concern in our culture, so much so that we all share certain beliefs about fat people. The very existence of these beliefs demonstrates that body size carries for us great meaning. If asked to describe a fat person, similar in every way except weight to a thin person, people describe the fat person as less likeable, less competent, less kind, less interesting, less successful. Thin people have a better chance of getting a job and getting into college, and they are generally hired at a higher starting salary. No wonder we worry so much about weight. Who wants to live with the stereotype our culture holds of fat people? Who wants to confront such outright discrimination?

When I lead a "Body Image and Self-Esteem Group," the heavy women, once they feel safe, can speak candidly about their pain at thinking of themselves as fat. They know that when they walk into the room, people sometimes stare at them or unobtrusively scan them from head to toe, thinking to themselves, "How could she let herself get so fat?" These women know that they wiggle as they walk, that they wear clothes such as beltless shifts or long overblouses to hide their bodies, that they avoid mirrors that show anything below the neck, and that they detest having their pictures taken. Some heavy women avoid relationships with men if they're single or avoid having sex with their husbands if they're not.

Women, particularly in adolescence, are punished for obesity. For a teenage girl, to be overweight is to be teased or ignored by the boys. Well-meaning friends criticize her ("if only you'd lose weight") or "manage" her, suggesting diets or dress styles to make her look thinner, or attempting to encourage her by saying, "You have such a pretty face." If a boy is overweight, he generally does not see himself as unattractive and often can excel in other ways, such as sports. (Think of the Chicago Bears' 300-pound William "Refrigerator" Perry.) A teenage girl is usually praised for thinness, even for extreme thinness, whereas a too-thin teenage boy is criticized for being effeminate and weak.

This bias against heavy women continues into adulthood. If a man marries a thin woman, his friends congratulate him on catching "such a looker!" Heavy women are less likely to be hired or promoted at work. With increased options for women in the workplace, why is it that we seem to have only one option for body size or shape? A "body beautiful" can be slim or chunky, tall or short.

Many of these biases are so deeply embedded in our culture that they have come to shape our own perceptions without our awareness. We need to acknowledge our assumptions about and reactions to heavy people in order to understand our own fear of fat.

How many of these statements do you agree with?

☐ Obese people have undesirable personality characteristics.
☐ Obese people have emotional problems.
☐ Obese people are gluttons.
☐ Obesity is necessarily unhealthy.
☐ You can choose to be any weight you want.

All these are myths—myths widely held. Let's look at them one by one.

MYTH: Obese people have undesirable personality characteristics. Despite our expectations, there are no particular character traits consistently associated with fatness. Obese people are no more jolly, or irresponsible, or lazy, or motherly. Nor are obese people more sinful than the rest of us.

Indeed, compulsive dieters may show neurotic characteristics far beyond those of obese people. These people are called compulsive because they are driven to dieting by obsessive thoughts—for example, that food is always fattening and eating is sinful. One compulsive dieter who has written me for years always starts her letter with a description of what she had for dinner the night before. This may be an extreme example, but eating dominates the thoughts and lives of compulsive eaters and dieters and makes them less pleasant to be around.

MYTH: Obese people have emotional problems. This myth is similar to, but more destructive than, the earlier myth and is also consistent with our beliefs about thinness and goodness. If thin is good, then fat is bad. In our culture, uncomfortable with terms like "good" and "evil," we substitute the language of psychology, so we learn that to be fat is to be "neurotic" and that obese people have extreme "oral needs." We imagine all fat people are emotionally needy. Yet obese people are no more likely to have emotional problems than thin people and those who do have emotional problems do not share a common diagnosis.[2] They experience the same range of emotions and diagnoses as nonobese people. Obese people, as a group, cannot be stereotyped as any more needy or emotional or immature or orally fixated than the rest of us.

The truly emotionally needy are those who are chaotic eaters. And *they* come in all shapes and sizes.

MYTH: Obese people are gluttons. Most of us assume that obese people eat more than they need. "If they just had self-control . . ." we say, implying that their lack of self-control makes them fat. Yet heavy people do not necessarily eat more food at each sitting, eat more quickly, or eat more frequently than nonobese people. Episodes of overeating, that is, eating far beyond satiety, occur as frequently in all types of eating-troubled people, regardless of one's size. In addition, the metabolism of many heavy people works against their efforts to lose weight by maintaining their heavy weight at a stable level.

Obese people may be less active than thin people, because they report that vigorous movement takes too much effort, too much strain.[3] Our culture, however, is much more critical of people who are fat than those who don't exercise. Indeed, despite the evidence that exercise enhances physical health and longevity, many people choose a lifestyle of inactivity.

It seems that some obese people have more sensitive smell and taste than do people of "normal" weight.[4] External cues stimulate their appetites. They may be more likely to eat by the clock or to eat when food is presented. In this way, obese people act very much like dieters or people who are starving. People who are attempting to eat less food than their body needs are more sensitive to external food cues. They may experience enhanced hunger and eat beyond satiety when food is available.

Obesity is often seen as evidence of gluttony, one of the seven deadly sins. In Dante's *Inferno*, there is a ring of hell devoted to gluttons. Yet, the Scriptures focus on attitudes, not on a specific characteristic such as weight. First Timothy 6:8 says, "If we have food and clothing, we will be content with that." Gluttony is an attitude toward food, not achieving a certain body weight. One can be thin or fat and still be subject to gluttony: the discontent, the obsessive preoccupation with food that underlies compulsive eating and dieting.

MYTH: Obesity is necessarily unhealthy. We assume that the thinner one is, the healthier. This is not necessarily true. Several recent studies have shown that weighing too much *or* too little can shorten a person's life.[5] Thus, being too thin can be as much of a health risk as being too fat. Instead of saying, "You look so thin and healthy," we should say, "You look so average-weight and healthy!"

The risk of dying from overweight, even among men, has been greatly oversold.[6] Contrary to the popular belief that, as one gets heavier, mortality increases, mortality increases with either extreme under or overweight. Not until a woman is forty percent over her desirable weight should she begin to worry. Thus, using the Fogarty Table of Desirable Weights, a woman who is 5'4" (average weight 120 pounds) should not worry about weight until she is above 168 pounds; one who is 5'8" (average weight 136 pounds), above 190 pounds.[7] This is a wide range, and makes our obsession over losing five or ten pounds look foolish.

"Those last five pounds" that we obsess about may be the very pounds that *increase* our risk of health problems. On the average, one is healthier slightly above her goal weight than if one has achieved her goal.

Many researchers have come to agree that health risks do not accompany mild obesity. Moderate to severe obesity may contribute to the development of such disorders as adult onset diabetes and osteoarthritis, but obesity does not appear to be a cause of high blood pressure, coronary heart disease or cholesterol levels. It can *complicate* these health problems, and if one has these factors, one should consider losing weight for these reasons.[8] Further, being overweight in addition to hypertension is a known risk factor, particularly for men. But in the absence of these problems, being overweight, particularly mildly, is not a clear health risk.

Indeed, our stereotypes of obesity may contribute to health problems. Our negative expectations of obese people surely cause stress, driving women to the extremes of liposuction, stomach bypasses, and wiring their jaws shut. And stress, as we know, can actually contribute to physical illness. What's really unhealthy, then, is our obsession with an ideal of beauty that is physically unrealistic.

MYTH: You can choose to be any weight you want. Although most of our biological characteristics—height, skin color, and eye color—are recognized as outside of our control, weight is considered a choice. We stigmatize overweight people, blaming them for their weight. "My, you've let yourself get fat," the mother of one of my young adult clients recently said. We feel sorry for them that they cannot "control" their weight. Yet it would be odd to say, "My, you've let yourself get tall." Despite recent evidence that weight is largely genetically influenced, our language reveals our assumption that weight is a choice.

The belief that we can choose to be whatever weight we want has led to an unrealistic standard of thinness for women in our culture. Most people aim for a weight that is too low for their biological preprogramming to comfortably achieve. When we try to eat too little, our body thinks it is starving and tries to compensate. Rare is the person who can stay on a strict diet for very long, or who can return to the same diet over and over.

In fact, if weight is biological, like height, we should expect some people to be at the extremes. Some people are unusually tall or short. Some people are very dark, others more light in skin color. We accept this without question; yet we act as if the average-weight person is normal, and extremely fat or thin people, abnormal.

In contrast to the widely held myth that we can choose our body size, recent studies indicate that one's weight is strongly genetically influenced. Children's weight is much like their parents. It is true that parents affect their children's weight by the eating experiences they provide: what they give their children to eat, how much, how often, and in what context. Yet, when the effects of experiences are controlled (for example, by studying children raised in families other than their birth families), parental weight and shape are more highly correlated than any other factor with their children's weight and shape. Set point theory, the relative proportion of one's fat and thin cells, metabolic rate—all describe possible genetic influences on weight. One may *contribute* to obesity by eating habits, exercise, and emotional confusions, but there is no known nongenetic *cause* of obesity.

In other words, sitting in front of the television munching on pretzels because your children no longer need you may make you fatter, but only as you fight against, ignore, or overwhelm your body's natural response of hunger. Conversely, an active lifestyle and self-nurturant eating can mediate a tendency to become fat, only if one's weight is comfortably within one's set point range.

Dieting Is Unhealthy

"Quick-Fix Swimsuit Diet—Melt Away 10 lbs. in 7 Days!" screams a headline in the *Star*. Not to be outdone, the *National Examiner* proclaims: "Lose 15 lbs. in 5 days." Just in case you miss the reason for these diets, another headline in the *Star* reads, "My friend Brenda the Blimp has a backside like a wrecking ball."

Diets are big business, and although we spend millions of dollars on them yearly, *diet programs*—particularly these that are sensationalized in the supermarket tabloids, but also programs sold in your local bookstore and advertised in your local newspaper—are poorly monitored, often based on faulty reasoning, and may be risky for your health. For example, the Beverly Hills Diet does not even provide basic nutritional requirements.[9] The authors of this diet argue that one should eat from only one of the basic four food groups because limiting intake to one food group contributes to metabolic changes and favors weight loss. There is no evidence for positive benefits from eating from only one food group, and there is strong evidence that nutrients from each of the four food groups contribute to better physical functioning.

Another recent review of nine diet books, chosen because they appeared in the health, fitness, and diet sections of local bookstores, similarly documented nutritional deficiencies in popular diet programs. Only fifteen percent of menus provided sufficient servings from the four basic food groups. None of the diets met recommended levels for vitamins and minerals, even with nutritional supplements. None of the diets recommended iron supplements, and seven failed to provide adequate iron requirements, especially since women in their childbearing years, with high needs for iron, are the most likely to be on a diet. Only two of the nine reviewed were considered reasonable diets. One of these two recommended exercise in combination with moderate eating, since exercise is known to produce physiological benefits that modulate appetite. Several of the other diets recommended exercise, but their advice was un-sound—for example, they failed to recommend adequate nutrients to support exercise safely. The lay consumer, un-trained as a nutritionist, is unable to make these same evaluations and is at risk for health problems as a result.[10]

Weight loss programs such as Optifast and Nutri-System, advertised as more comprehensive than diet programs, gener-ally sell special foods and encourage a changed lifestyle. They are quite expensive, yet do not provide long-term, successful solutions for eating problems. Ninety-five percent of those on weight-loss programs regain their weight within two years. This is particularly true of quick weight-loss programs. A truism in the weight-loss business is "the quicker you lose, the sooner you gain." Your body does not adjust well to rapidly changing intake, maintains its original level of need, and demands more food until you feed it.

These weight-loss programs may be dangerous to your health. As this book goes to press, Nutri-System, an extremely popular weight-loss system based on a strict regimen of exercise and a diet of foods primarily marketed by Nutri-System, is being sued for contributing to gallbladder problems. Although they claim to have been approved by the American Medical Association, American Heart Association, American Dietetic Association, and American Diabetes Association, at least three of these organizations have asked that Nutri-System stop using their names in advertising. Fad diets, liquid diets, and other extreme weight-loss techniques may also be danger-ous to your health and should never be attempted without a doctor's supervision.

In general, restrictive eating programs—by far the most common techniques for weight loss—tend to provide initial weight loss but cannot help women maintain a lowered weight. Your body is hungry, and you know it. Later, when you no longer restrict, your body makes up for its earlier deprivation. Dieting, then, contributes to overeating, and later weight gain.

Healthful eating begins with a willingness to give up dieting, eat reasonably, and exercise moderately.

Group weight loss programs, such as Take Off Pounds Sensibly (TOPS) and Weight Watchers, are also based on a restriction model, which interfere with the development of satisfying eating programs. They do sometimes "work," in that they can break long-established overeating patterns and help reduce weight, and the benefits of peer support are not to be ignored. But, for them to "work," one usually has to follow an eating paradigm for the rest of one's life. In other words, one chooses "abnormal" eating. Further, many who participate feel themselves controlled by or addicted to the program. Rather than encouraging autonomy and independence, these programs foster dependence on the group. They encourage one to fill one's time with group meetings and friendships with other members of the group. They define the member as forever "abstinent," rather than "cured," contributing to feelings of powerlessness and dependency. In a weight-loss program based on an addiction model, such as Overeaters Anonymous, followers admit that they are powerless to control their eating. They propose that one must become abstinent from overeating or from self-defined problem foods. While the twelve-step programs may be appropriate for controlling compulsions that are self-destructive, dangerous, or part of a disease process, eating is another story, because eating is an essentially nourishing process, necessary for life.

Restriction and addiction models blame the woman for overeating and offer her salvation through a particular diet or through avoidance. She is taught not to trust her own body and instead gives control over to an external authority. Dependence on the group and its structure usually becomes necessary for continued abstinence. Addiction and restriction models put power in external sources and thus contribute to women's sense of helplessness and low self-esteem. In contrast, a self-nurturing model teaches women to trust their own bodies and frees them to live their lives without constant external measure.

Christian weight programs, additionally, may spiritualize

thinness, making it a major criterion for spiritual victory. "Thinness is next to godliness" could be their rallying cry, and someone who is thin is seen as having good discipline and as being obedient to the will of God.

Consider the personal story of Joan Cavanaugh, told in *More of Jesus, Less of Me,* one of several diet books found in Christian bookstores.[11] Although her problems with eating are real, and not to be trivialized, her theology contributes to mind/body dualism. Her title and her story suggest that thin Christians are more spiritual, and the thinner the better. Eating too much is described as sin, and dieting as obedience to God. Christians perpetuate societal myths, dieting just as strenuously as those who diet for more worldly reasons. Indeed, one may feel more guilt for violating one's diet if God is seen as the originator of the diet.

Fasting is a spiritual discipline that is sometimes confused with dieting. Fasting was encouraged in the Old Testament and practiced by Jesus as a way of recognizing God's sovereignty in our lives. Jesus never directly prescribed or advocated fasting, although he did comment that it should not be done for self-glorification. Practiced appropriately, fasting can be an important means by which we focus on God.

Fasting is, however, easily misused, particularly by those who already experience chaotic eating and confusions about weight. Fasting to lose weight gives religious meaning to an act that is actually selfishly inspired. Those who fast will receive spiritual and social rewards from their peers that encourage them to continue the practice and make it increasingly difficult for them to acknowledge their confusions. For this reason, spiritual disciplines other than fasting are more beneficial for those with eating concerns.

Focus on Eating, Not on Fat

In our weight-obsessed culture, there are positive indications that attitudes toward weight are changing: chic fashions for heavier women, the success of Roseanne Barr Arnold and

Oprah Winfrey, the founding of the Fat Is Beautiful Society. Yet too many of us allow our attitudes to continue to be shaped by "fat-ism," our outright prejudice against heavy people.

For too long we have judged ourselves by the size of our bodies because we have believed that being fat was sinful, neurotic, and ugly. We have sought to obtain and maintain thinness with weight-loss strategies that are ineffective and self-destructive. We need to shift our focus from "I'm thin; I'm fat" judgments to realistic evaluations of our eating behaviors. We eat wrongly when we eat chaotically, unresponsive to our body and its needs.

Millions of women are literally making themselves ill as they struggle to conform to the destructive ideals of thinness. No one suffers more from these ideal-versus-real discrepancies than women who are bulimic or anorexic. Let's first consider the plight of the bulimic—the ultimate yo-yo dieter.

3.

Bulimia: The Secret Millions Share

Lois is regarded by her peers as having everything: good looks, intelligence, spiritual sensitivity, lots of dates, and a good job. But Lois lives a dual life. On the average of three times a week, Lois stuffs herself with whatever sweet and crunchy food she can find. Afterward she panics and makes herself vomit, comforting herself that the calories are gone and she can have control over her eating again. She plans to eat lightly at dinner, perhaps a salad and diet soft drink. She keeps her "binge" life a secret from even her closest friends. She sees herself as weak and sinful and doubts that God can love her.

Bulimia is the technical term for this cycle of dieting, binge eating, and purging. It is a more common problem than any of us wants to believe, even in Christian circles. If you are bulimic, you are not alone. Bulimia was rare before the 1960s but now could be considered a national epidemic among young adults. Bulimia is practiced by eight percent of high school seniors and up to twenty percent of college seniors. Bulimia is not limited to teenagers. When questionnaires were given out at a shopping mall, over ten percent of all women shoppers reported bulimic symptoms at some time in their lives.[1] As many as 7.6 million American women may share the "binge-purge" secret. It is likely that every one of us knows well at least one person—a friend, a girl in the church youth group, the daughter of good friends, or our own daughter—who is actively bulimic. Some of us know several bulimic women and may be well aware of how greatly it affects their lives.

Men are not as susceptible to bulimia as women. Only five to ten percent of known bulimics are men, although this may underestimate the actual count because men are less likely to seek help for bulimia. Some men who practice bulimia may want quick weight reduction for occupational purposes such as wrestling, riding in horseraces, or long-distance running. As a society we can tolerate larger body size in men, especially if muscles accompany heaviness, so that men experience less pressure to control eating. As physical fitness and weight consciousness become priorities for men, distorted and chaotic eating patterns are increasingly common in men. For these men, the psychological roots of bulimia are the same as they are for women, and the solutions we recommend are relevant to male as well as female bulimics.

The "Wheel of Misfortune"

Bulimia traps one in a "wheel of misfortune," a repetitive cycle of dieting, bingeing, and purging. If you are bulimic, you probably focus on either the binge or the purge as the problem. But bulimia's three phases intertwine in complicated and powerful ways. Each phase of the cycle must be addressed before the pattern can be broken. In essence, to overcome bulimia, you must stop dieting, stop bingeing, and stop purging, all at the same time. To stop purging without altering other points in the cycle won't cure bulimia.

The Diet Phase

Dieting starts and ends the bulimic cycle. A person on a diet is striving for control of her appetite, of her body, and of almost everything in her life. Dieting seems a way to perfection. A thin body will ensure the perfect relationship and the perfect life. She expects dieting to have good effects such as getting her a boyfriend, helping her feel competent, or giving her a sense of spiritual victory. But dieting in and of itself cannot produce these personal changes. These false expectations motivate the dieting, and dieting feels good—as long as it lasts. But "successful" dieting over the long term is impossible for bulimic women. Even when they realize this, they do not give up dieting. For women with bulimia, dieting gives way to bingeing, which leads them to purge in an effort to beat their biology: to eat without absorbing calories. The cycle works through these pathways:[2]

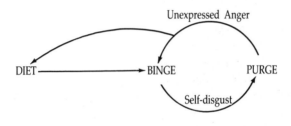

DIET	BINGE	PURGE
Strive for perfection	Here and now	Fear of fat
Struggle for control	Union of body and mind	Mind over body
High expectations	Loss of self-awareness	Future perfection

The Binge

For a bulimic woman, dieting triggers binge eating.[3] The pressure of the diet sooner or later swings into a binge—eating a relatively large amount of food in a relatively short period of time. What constitutes a binge depends on what food is off-limits to the individual woman. For a woman on a grapefruit diet, three peanut butter cookies can be a binge. But binges commonly consist of women eating large amounts—a package of cookies, a half gallon of ice cream, a bag of tortilla chips, and all the leftover chicken in the refrigerator. Bulimics may find themselves shoplifting snack food to meet their impulsive urge to eat. Bingeing can be a brief experience, over in half an hour while waiting for the school bus to bring the children home. Or binge eating can be a long, slow, nonstop process, in which a woman nibbles all evening on crackers, nuts, leftover Chinese food, and teaspoons of pudding. Once the overeating starts, and the woman violates her restrictions, she may feel she has "blown it" and it doesn't matter what she eats now. She tells herself she will go back on her diet tomorrow.

For a woman with bulimia, the binge is an intense, focused experience during which she is absorbed in the here-and-now experience of the food in her mouth: its smoothness, its saltiness, its crackle. There is a sense of abandonment to immediate, pleasurable physical sensations. She can stifle that voice of conscience, block those fears, ignore those uncomfortable feelings with just one more Oreo cookie. After the restrictions of dieting, the "out of control" sensation feels good enough to be addictive. The compulsion to "have that potato chip right now" eliminates objectivity and self-awareness. One feels reduced to a large open mouth because, during a binge, nothing else matters but what is felt in the mouth. It is a moment of intense pleasure, even euphoria, but it doesn't last long enough.

After the binge comes the crash. Overeating stops, usually not because the woman chooses to stop, but because the food is gone, or the children come home, or she is in pain from eating too much. Occasionally she may eat herself into a stupor that gives way to sleep. Inevitably, the mouth experience gives way to the mind experience of despair and misery. All bulimics share an intense horror of calories and fat following a binge and become overwhelmed by feelings of panic, self-disgust, and guilt. One woman could visualize the food being churned up in her stomach and the calories transforming themselves into fat cells. She "hated" them and felt that they had to be punished, exorcised, shriveled up, or worn out by exercise. It is the power of this emotional experience—the fear, the anger, the panic— that leads into the purging phase of the cycle.

The Purge

Self-disgust compels the bulimic woman to take severe, self-abusive measures to rid herself of the food as quickly as possible. She must, at all costs, regain a sense of control by subduing her body. Self-induced vomiting dramatizes a woman's desperate attempt to control her panic at having all those calories inside.

> *Laura was an experienced ten-year bulimic who visualized her body ballooning up around her until it almost reached the bursting point if she did not purge. She eventually built vomiting into her daily schedule, and at her worst point, vomited as much as seventeen times a day. She used to say that the only problem in self-induced vomiting is finding the time and place to do it. Laura was so good at disguising her behavior that her housemate suspected nothing unusual for over a year. Like all habitual vomiters, she began to isolate herself, choosing to give up friendships rather than face the constant threat of embarrassment if her friends found out about her "disgusting habit."*

Women try to counter the aftereffects of binge eating by taking laxatives, diuretics, syrup of ipecac, or cathartics which bring on diarrhea, excessive urination, or vomiting. In so doing, women try to eliminate food faster than calories can be absorbed into the body. People who find it difficult or distasteful to vomit may feel that taking medicine is easier and safer. It seems to provide a quick fix, and is comforting to those who believe that the answer to every problem comes in a pill or bottle. All they actually give themselves is a nasty bout of nausea, intestinal distress, and hours in the bathroom. Laxative abuse does not inhibit caloric absorption to any significant degree. Use of these chemicals is extremely dangerous, because it so abruptly shifts the natural chemical-fluid balance in the body. Those addicted to laxative abuse often increase the amount of medicine they take because they wrongly assume that the more they use, the faster and more thoroughly calories leave their system.

The third common strategy for purging is severe dieting, usually accompanied by vigorous exercise. The bulimic woman vows to redeem herself by sheer willpower. Kate typically refused all food for two days postbinge and engaged in massive doses of exercise—running, aerobics, hours on the Nautilus equipment. She envisioned herself cutting off chunks of the fat cells that might have been plumped up by her caloric binge. Kate perceived the fasting as control, but it was illusory control because it always led her back into a binge. At other times it felt like penance for bingeing, a form of self-punishment.

Some women experience the purge as ugly, but necessary for relief. Other women experience the purge as a positive, cleansing process. When I asked Antonia how it felt to be vomiting out in the woods alone after a binge, I expected to hear her pain. Instead she said that it felt wonderful, and she felt gloriously hopeful when she was vomiting. For Antonia the purge was a ritual cleansing, a chance to wipe out her sinfulness so that she could start living in a purer way. She thought of her self-induced vomiting metaphorically as redemption after the sinful binge. This illusion of redemption, this sensation of getting right with God, may make it difficult for a Christian woman to give up purging. The purge is counterfeit cleansing; it does not change a person from within. Because the purge is self-destructive, it actually adds to the guilt and pain of the bulimic.

Purging doesn't work. The purge cannot meet the bulimic's hope of letting her eat without calories. During a binge, calories flow into the bulimic's body. And no method of purging, not even immediate vomiting, can eliminate all the calories. Purging may actually encourage overeating. When a woman believes she can lose most of the calories by purging, she feels free to eat, particularly if she finds it easier to purge on a full stomach. Purging by any method is therefore misleading, encouraging overeating without eliminating the calories.

Can It Really Hurt You?

Absolutely. Bulimia destroys bodies. The physical effects immediately after the binge are obvious: feelings of nausea, fatigue, stomach pain, and bloating. But the long-term effects of bulimia are more serious.[4] Some women develop swelling, pain, and tenderness of the salivary and parotid glands in the neck. About fifty percent of women who are bulimic develop menstrual disturbances, irregularity or loss of periods. Recurrent vomiting causes irreversible erosion of dental enamel and may produce chronic hoarseness of the voice. Women who abuse laxatives may lose bowel reactivity and feel constipated, so they take more laxatives, until their system can no longer function normally.

Bulimia throws the body into metabolic chaos. It disturbs the balance of body fluids, so that the woman alternates between water retention and dehydration. Recurrent dehydration produces dry skin, dizziness, constant thirst, and brittleness of hair and nails. Almost fifty percent of bulimic women show electrolyte imbalance, which contributes to metabolic disturbances, kidney dysfunction, or epileptic seizures. Hypokalemia, or loss of potassium in the body, may cause irregular heartbeats or other severe cardiac problems that may result in death. The good news is that, except for more extreme or long-term cases, these problems generally resolve once the bulimic behavior ceases.

Many clients with bulimia cannot see the diet-binge-purge cycle in their own lives. When they can recognize the pattern, or if they learn of the dangers of practicing bulimia, they may decide to do something about it. Unfortunately, some may recognize the cycle that controls their life but feel they have no other option for achieving their goals. Dr. Craig Johnson notes that those ten percent of women with bulimia who say that they are unwilling to gain five to ten pounds in exchange for stopping their binge eating, purging, or food preoccupation have more difficulty making progress in controlling their disorder.[5] These bulimics feel that bulimia is the only thing that has helped them to stay as thin as they want, and they determine to be thin at all costs. Even the high costs of bulimia—the dangers to physical health, the erosion of self-esteem, and the alienation from God—do not seem too high.

How Does It Start?

Women with bulimia do not possess a single character flaw, have a certain type of mother, or share a single gene that brings on bulimic symptoms. Girls who appear to be developing normally may develop the disorder without anyone realizing what is happening. But the roots of the disorder can begin very early in life.

Most teenage girls go on a diet, often early in puberty. At this time, their bodies are laying down new fat deposits that will make childbearing possible, yet they resist this natural process, feeling weight gain is unacceptable and must be controlled. Dieting at this critical growth time causes chaos in metabolic regulation. Girls are hungry, even starving, and they do not listen to their body's needs. They struggle instead to be thin, and as a result of continued dieting and of pubertal changes they need to take stronger and stronger measures to prevent weight gain.

Susan and Bruce Wooley have put it this way:

> *Dieting and management of the effects of starvation thus become the fabric of a young woman's life into which new threads may be gradually woven: the receipt of special attention; a safe means of expressing aggression; the means to control feelings of "goodness" and "badness" through manipulation of a single behavior; and above all, the conviction that through her suffering she will eventually achieve something of inestimable value. That the antici-pated external rewards never materialize is scarcely no-*

ticed, for they have been supplanted by internal ones and the unshakeable belief that triumph is just a few more pounds away. The original reasons for dieting are long forgotten, and the capacity for normal pleasures is wholly lost; the process has become an end in itself.[6]

Girls may learn to purge from each other. They hear about purging techniques from friends and the media, and with a little practice it may become easy to do on a daily basis. The ability to purge frees them to eat openly because they feel they can empty themselves at will.

Not all teenagers are trapped by the promise of purging. Some girls are more vulnerable than others, as a result of complicated emotional needs and past histories. Some find in bulimia a "secret" that makes them feel important; some find a safe way to express anger; some feel less lonely and isolated; and some find it helpful in coping with parental pressure. Gradually women come to believe that purging is the only way to immediately control their weight gain after those moments of emotionally driven eating. The constant dieting is impossible for them, probably because of their natural set point. But they believe that bulimia works for them: it keeps them thinner than they'd be if they really gave in and enjoyed their food all the time.

The Family Context of Bulimia

Women with bulimia often feel trapped in their family circle. A young woman is growing up and trying to assert herself as an independent individual, but in the context of a family that may be too close, these normal processes may be stifled.

Christine, a thirty-three-year-old single woman, worked as an artist in a variety of exciting settings. Although many of her artistic ventures had been successful, and she had moved all around the country, she kept coming back home periodically to live. Her bulimic symptoms often increased just before she made the decision to return home and contributed to her perceived need for the safety of home. But at home her daily struggles with her mother about her eating only made her dieting, bingeing, and purging more extreme until she felt compelled to address her eating dilemmas in a more direct, therapeutic way. Christine felt like a little girl, caught by trying to be everything her mother and father wanted her to be even though the expectations were conflicting: be successfully independent, but be dependent on us.

Often bulimic girls are model children. They conform to other people's expectations of them, rather than behaving and judging themselves by any internal standards of their own value. They try to do everything perfectly. When rejection comes—and it always does—the girls cannot cope with it, because they have no clear sense of who they are inside. So they turn their attention to their body size, which they feel more able to control. These girls need parents who can credibly challenge the peer/social pressures for thinness without demanding conformity. Within the family context of safety, teenagers need encouragement to define themselves, to express their feelings, and to set goals for themselves.

Bulimic behavior is grotesque and self-abusive. Bingeing and purging often substitute for experiencing and expressing anger. Making oneself throw up, have diarrhea, or starve are powerful, primitive, and ugly behaviors. One teenager explained that when her mother would criticize her she would binge because she was unhappy and then, focusing on her anger at her mother, she would vomit to make her mother unhappy. Turning her anger inward against her own body seemed safer than expressing it directly. The bulimic often internalizes gripes, swallows complaints, and eats criticism—only to throw it all up. Confusions and concerns which should be addressed directly get channeled into this futile quest, this constant struggle for control of eating. As a woman acknowledges anger, she can use its energy to produce change in her life and relationships.

Bulimic women often grow up in families where mothers, grandmothers, and even great-grandmothers have been obsessed with being thin or being beautiful. Some reports suggest that sixty percent of mothers of bulimics are themselves afraid of being fat.[7] One woman with an eating problem recalled this experience:

> I was about four years old when I went with my mother to a Memorial Day parade. I was enjoying it immensely until my mother leaned over and told me to take a good look at that majorette who had elephant thighs. "She shouldn't be allowed to march in a parade showing off those disgusting legs. Don't ever let yourself look like that."

This child learned early a deep-seated fear of fat. Most of us learn in dozens of direct and indirect ways that being slender is better. Family members of bulimics often share distorted attitudes about food, eating, dieting, and body image.

Breaking the unspoken tradition demanding thinness or mandating anxiety about food may require some research into your family of origin. Begin by asking questions, like those listed in the "Family Roots of Eating" exercise, of women in your family. Perhaps bringing these hidden expectations to light and discussing the sources of these values will shift your own attitude and release you from living out these multigenerational agendas.

Exercise:
Family
Roots of
Eating

1. Ask your mother, grandmother, aunts, and sisters about their histories of eating and weight concerns—as a child, an adolescent, premarriage, as a mother, postmenopause, and now.

2. How does she describe her past attitudes and actions from her current perspective? How

did the fashions of her times affect her attitudes toward her body? How did her relationships affect her feelings of being attractive? How did the economics of her time or availability of food affect her eating?

3. If she could change something about her eating, her weight, or her body image and do it over again, what would she change?

4. What does she know about bulimia? Has she had eating/thinness/food issues? If she can admit her uncertainty or vulnerability it may be helpful for you to share your experiences with bulimia.

5. Compare her responses with your own. Any surprises? What can you learn that may be useful for you in your struggle?

What Can Be Done to Help?

Breaking free from bulimia requires a woman to simultaneously address restrictive dieting *and* binge eating *and* purging. Stopping any one symptom of the cycle is not enough. Giving up purging without stopping dieting does not solve this eating disorder and increases the likelihood of a return to full-blown bulimia during times of stress. Giving up binge eating is a nearly impossible goal unless one gives up restrictive dieting at the same time. For a woman with bulimia, any steps taken away from excessive dieting, uncontrolled binge eating, and premeditated purging are giant steps. Introducing a greater variety of foods into your eating choices, allowing yourself to eat forbidden foods, stopping a binge before the food runs out, or delaying a purge for half an hour are critical ways to learn to assert personal choices over your eating. The following two exercises are efforts to structure your reflections on the binge and purge dynamics within your own distinctive patterns.

Exercise:
Breaking the Binge

1. Anticipate a binge. Figure out what circumstances make it easy to binge. Does it occur on the weekends, in the evenings, when bored, when upset, at family occasions, when alone, when overly hungry, when already full, when certain foods are easily available? What is the trigger for this binge?

2. When you can identify that you are binge eating, take a moment to label it as a binge. Sit down, slow down, even write down what you are experiencing at that moment. Are you tasting the food? Are you enjoying it? What would you really like to eat?

3. Identify the feelings that led you to eating. Who were you thinking about?

4. What is the eating doing for you right now? Is it calming you? Is it producing oblivion? Is it filling up empty time and empty emotions? Is it distracting you from something painful?

5. What will happen if you stop eating and sit with your feelings? What could you do to act on your feelings in a productive way? Try to do so, even for a minute or two. For a compulsive eater the only way out of the destructive eating pattern is to get inside yourself and trust that there is a voice, a part of yourself that can inform you about what you really want emotionally. Listen to that voice.

6. Consider a list of alternative activities, even rewards for yourself to make it easier to break out of the current binge episode.

7. Call a friend, a confidante who knows about your binge pattern and can give you encouragement to deal constructively with your current eating crisis.

8. Recognize your feeling of fullness. After a binge, don't eat again until you feel hungry, but don't starve yourself into a position of being too hungry.

Exercise: **1.** Examine your personalized purge sequence
Overpowering in as detailed a way as possible.
the Purge
☐ What circumstances are likely to produce the desire to purge?
☐ When and where is the purge easy? What makes purging difficult?
☐ What is your body cue (ache, pain, pressure) that you want to purge?
☐ What are the repetitive thoughts or obsessional ideas that lead you to purge?
☐ How early in a binge do you know that you'll purge?
☐ Would your bingeing change if you decided during your binge definitely not to purge?
☐ How do you feel immediately after purging? How do you feel one hour after the purge? How do you feel about it the next day?

2. Don't phase out or tune out on the binge-purge connection. Pull yourself out of the fogginess of the purge experience by acknowledging to yourself what you are doing. Tell yourself honestly and directly that you can purge if you choose to—and you can choose not to purge.

3. Delay the purge for increased increments of time. Congratulate yourself for every ten minutes that passes postbinge without your taking purgative action. Don't use the delay of the purge to return to eating.

4. Decrease the intensity of the purge. Make fewer, less intense efforts to vomit during the purge; cut back gradually and consistently on the amount of laxatives you take; cut back fifteen minutes on your exercise routine.

5. Generate other alternatives to purging. What could you do that would decrease your need to purge? Post a list in the bathroom as a reminder of other coping strategies for the purging impulse.

6. Reward yourself for the effort you put into overpowering the purge. Recognize that any little success contributes to your long-term recovery.

Bulimia is a serious medical problem that requires professional attention. It is essential that a physician follow the medical condition of a woman with bulimia because the side effects of a bulimic lifestyle can be life-threatening. Yet many women with bulimia resist telling their doctors about their behavior, even when an examination shows menstrual disturbance or cardiac irregularities, because they feel embarrassed or fear hospitalization. Most doctors do not recommend hospitalization for a bulimic unless her physical condition puts her at risk, her depression is incapacitating, or her lifestyle or family situation is too chaotic to accommodate change.

Some clinicians view bulimia as a symptom of an underlying chemical depression and recommend medication. But the signs of depression (lethargy, difficulty concentrating, low feelings) may actually be a result of the physical effects of starving, bingeing, and purging. Antidepressants may have an initially positive effect on bulimic symptoms, perhaps because the woman feels more positive about her situation. For the most severe bulimics a medical intervention may provide the energy needed to start off the serious process of change. Medication does not seem to be effective in the long run unless the bulimic makes dramatic changes in the behavior, attitudes, relationships, and emotions that support the bulimic symptoms.

It is critical to find a community of caring. Tell your family and friends about your struggles with eating. Enlist their support in ways you specify as you take the steps necessary for recovery. Family and friends may provide you with realistic feedback about your eating behaviors that can help you see yourself more clearly. If they are not supportive of your process of change, find support within the wider community. Although self-help groups geared toward compulsive overeating, addictive habits, or children of dysfunctional families may not offer a sound or specific intervention plan for bulimia, they can provide a safe place, an open community in which to share your struggles to reconstruct your life. If you hear of bulimia support groups available in your community, either through the local mental health center, women's services center, or as an informal group, go to it and participate as fully as you can. Ask your local Christian counseling center to start a therapy group for Christian women with chaotic eating problems. Find a facilitator to start a discussion group, a Christian education series, or a prayer group about eating problems.

Bulimia may be complicated, but it is curable. Because bulimia is so complex it must be approached on multiple levels: eating behaviors, emotional undercurrents, relationship dilemmas, body anxieties, and embedded beliefs about thinness. Conviction, courage, and consistency are the three Cs that make it possible for a woman with bulimia to change. Conviction is the awareness that it is time to change NOW which motivates the efforts to eat differently. Courage gets one through the difficult times when the impulse to restrict, to binge, or to purge seems overwhelming. Consistency is provided by the plans, organization, and structures (like those recommended in this book) that define a path to follow through the complexity of the bulimic cycle. It takes a great deal of moral character, input from caring people, and trust in God to transform bulimic dieting, bingeing, and purging into satisfying eating. God honors every step we take toward wholeness and health.

4. Anorexia Nervosa: Dieting to Death

Janie, emaciated and gaunt, arrives home from school for the Christmas holidays. She has lost so much weight since the summer! Their good little Janie. But when they mention it to her, she refuses to talk about it, changing the subject. Janie has changed in other ways, too. She talks constantly about food and eating, and frequently volunteers to cook for the family. Yet, at mealtimes, she just pushes food around on her plate. She seems to be eating only white bread and nuts. She is harder to talk with than she used to be. She is more irritable, especially toward her mother, and everyone in the family feels she is more distant and moody than ever before. The family physician finds that she has stopped having her period and is anemic, and confirms that she has anorexia nervosa.

In the past twenty years, anorexia nervosa, the most dramatic and least common of the chaotic eating patterns, has received considerable media attention. It has been glamorized as a result, but Janie's family will quickly tell you that the reality is painful and tragic.

First described in the 1870s, anorexia occurred relatively rarely until the late 1950s, but since then has become increasingly common, probably as a result of increasing pressures toward thinness in women. Women with the fullblown disorder quickly become pathetic, emaciated beings who nevertheless assert that they are "too fat." Treatment is difficult and requires professionals experienced with the disorder and sometimes hospitalization. Some women eventually die of the disorder.

Who Has Anorexia?

Most anorexics (approximately ninety-five percent) are female. Anorexia in women begins most commonly in the teenage years (ages twelve to nineteen), when girls are struggling with issues of identity, separation from parents, intimacy, and sexuality. In their vulnerability, they begin trying to control eating, since everything else—relationships, school work, family—feels out of their control. But anorexia is not limited to teenagers. Girls as young as nine and women in their twenties and thirties can develop the disorder.

Little is known about male anorexics, but they seem to be similar to female anorexics and as difficult, if not more difficult, to treat. As with bulimia, men who suffer from the disorder are often trying to lose weight for sports, or to qualify for a certain career, such as jockey. They may also have a troubled relationship with their father. One male anorexic remembers eating only peas at one point in his life, when he was about six. He believes his anorexia began with struggling against his authoritarian father. Another anorexic male remembers his obsessive eating patterns beginning with a diet of pasta for breakfast, lunch, and dinner, in his efforts to get in shape for sports. Because anorexics are usually female, we will primarily address women in this chapter.

The *typical* anorexic is the introverted, conscientious, well-behaved, often second- or third-born girl in the family. She excels in school, in band, in whatever she tries, yet inside she feels like a failure. She often shops, cooks, sews, or otherwise cares for other family members. Families generally have only one anorexic member, but many mothers of anorexics worry excessively about their weight or are overly anxious and perfectionistic.

Anorexia is a pervasive disorder that affects the girl's sense of her identity. Friends and family report feeling that the anorexic has "changed so much that they hardly know her." The numbers of those suffering with the disorder are small, but its effects are dramatic: At least one percent of college women probably suffer from the disorder and some believe that as many as half a million people are anorexic. There is no evidence that anorexia nervosa is any less a problem among Christian families.

"I Am Still Too Fat": The Symptoms

"I cannot diet too much." In many cases, anorexia begins with a diet, and for this reason anorexia has sometimes been called the "dieter's disease." But the anorexic is not a typical dieter because dieting is relatively easy for her. Her "fear of fat" becomes an obsession, and her dieting continues far beyond the point of safety. As one anorexic woman said, "Being fat is more painful to me than struggling to be thin." She may develop bizarre eating patterns; for example, she may force herself to eat nothing but crackers and lettuce and to drink nothing but diet caffeine drinks. As the disorder continues, she may exercise obsessively and eat only in private. Her excuses for not participating in family or group meals are individually quite plausible but soon seem too frequent and glib.

"I don't feel hungry." The word "anorexia" literally means loss of appetite, but this is a misnomer. Anorexia is motivated by a fear of gaining weight, not by an absence of hunger. Although sufferers often deny that they are hungry or that they want to lose weight, recovering anorexics will admit that they always felt hungry but that they did not allow themselves to eat. "Better waste than waist," they say, and "The thinner is the winner," using slogans to spur themselves to further dieting. One anorexic reports that she put leftover ice cream in the trash can and covered it with cat litter to be sure that she would not go back to the trash can later and eat the ice cream.

"I am still too fat." Although some will deny their self-perceptions, anorexics diet obsessively because they perceive themselves as fat, even when they are dangerously thin. At 5'6"

and ninety pounds, Adrian described her frustration at limiting her intake to two muffins in a day and looking down at her stomach to find it still "sticking out." Anorexics consistently overestimate their body size.[1] When they look in the mirror, they see themselves as fat; when they draw pictures of themselves, they draw themselves as fat. Even though other women may wrongly describe themselves as fat, the anorexic's self-perception is extreme, unrealistic, and frustratingly difficult to change, even in the face of overwhelming evidence to the contrary.

"I cannot lose weight fast enough." To be diagnosed anorexic, a woman must lose at least twenty percent of her original body weight or be at least twenty percent below the expected weight for her height or age. Most anorexics stop menstruating. My anorexic clients tell me at what weight they lose their periods and can manipulate their weight to maintain or lose menstruation. For this reason, some experts believe that anorexia represents a fear of sexuality.

Unlike most people who are starving to death, however, anorexics may show a high energy level, running several miles a day or sleeping for shorter periods of time. Colleen, a woman with long-term anorexia, runs five miles daily, even in the snow, and allows herself no more than three to five hours of sleep a night. At night, while others sleep, she feels guilty if she is not writing reports or preparing her lesson plans for her classes the next day. Cherry Boone O'Neill, daughter of Pat Boone, shared the story of her struggle with anorexia in her book *Starving for Attention*. She said that "following my schedule from dawn to dusk would have made an Olympic trainer feel right at home. . . . The only feature of this Spartan schedule that an aspiring world-class athlete might find out of place would be the conspicuous absence of the all-important 'training table.' "[2]

"Sometimes my willpower is not enough." Anorexics may include extreme measures in their repertoire of ways to keep losing weight, such as self-induced vomiting. Unlike bulimics, anorexics do not usually feel in conflict, pain, or distress about

their destructive and restrictive eating behaviors. They tend to distort reality about their thinness so that they can deny feeling anxious about their health. Anorexics need others in their life to point out over and over again the reality that their restrictive eating and purging is extreme and dangerous. One anorexic described lying down on the floor when she felt dizzy from undereating; another drank so much tomato juice with pepper in it, to stave off feelings of hunger, that she developed ulcers.

"My life feels out of control." Ellen, at 5'8" and 108 pounds, talked each week in therapy about feeling fat and ugly and deciding—again!—to have yogurt for lunch. After recording when she most felt these feelings, she began to realize that she had telescoped an overwhelming sense of being out of control in her life into fat feelings. She could easily chronicle the crises of her life: Her sixteen-year-old daughter has started getting drunk regularly and refusing to come home for curfew; her boss is angry with her work and threatening to fire her; her income is too low to pay the rent; and her friends are unavailable when she needs them. When she began to deal directly with these issues, beginning with the easiest, one step at a time, she found that her feelings of being fat and ugly became less frequent.

One Christian with the diagnosis of anorexia admits that dieting has become a way of life, giving her a sense of purpose and making her feel in control. Not to diet is to lose her sense of self, a terrifying alternative. This same anorexic, upon finding she has gained a few much-needed pounds, writes, "I don't want people to see me. I feel ashamed. I am losing the identity I had with slimness. I don't want to live if I am chunky."

The anorexic girl in *Kessa*, a novel by Steven Levenkron, was asked if she missed being thin. She replied, "The other day I was looking in the mirror . . . I looked so bland—so nothing. Like anybody else. None of my chest bones showed. I used to love to feel all my bones."[3]

Some anorexics suffer such despair over their constant struggle to be in control of their own lives that they look forward to death. As Alex, a Christian with anorexia, writes, "It seems too futile going on. I wish that I could die from some complication of anorexia because then it would not be like I had deliberately taken action. If there is a God of mercy and compassion, may He allow me to die and another of greater and better potential be allowed to remain."

The Roots of the Sickness

Anorexia has multiple causes—biological, societal, familial and personal. Psychotherapist Hilde Bruch describes the typical anorexic family as one in which the child's needs are subordinate to the family's. The result is an overly conforming child without a clear sense of her own identity, except as it is expressed in her anorexia. Jessie is a fourteen-year-old girl, active in her church youth group. She sits with her mother in church on Sunday mornings and, when asked her opinion, quotes her mother or gives an opinion with which her mother would agree. When asked what *she* thinks, or what *she* wants, she cannot say.

Dr. Bruch opens her book *The Golden Cage* with this graphic quote from an anorexic patient, describing her sense of being a misfit in her own family and the mismatch between her sense of self and her family expectations: "She was like a sparrow in a golden cage, too plain and simple for the luxuries of her home, but also deprived of the freedom of doing what she truly wanted to do . . . cages are made for big colorful birds who show off their plumage and are satisfied just hopping around in the cage . . . she felt she was quite different, like a sparrow, inconspicuous and energetic, who wants to fly around and take off on its own, who is not made for a cage."[4]

Family therapist Stan Minuchin describes the typical family with an anorexic daughter as seemingly "perfect," with few conflicts.[5] In reality, he suggests, they ignore conflicts because they do not know how to resolve them. The mother and daughter are unusually close and cooperative. For brief periods, however, because their relationship is too close and the mother is overly involved in her daughter's life, the daughter becomes irritable and combative, arguing over issues that she would otherwise ignore. The father may be distant and little involved in family life. Both parents appear strong but are in actuality tired and needy. The child seems self-reliant and thus begins to take care of other family members, feeding them, shopping for them, listening to their pain, subjugating her own needs.

Jessie, the anorexic who lacked a strong sense of self, found her identity in the family until the normal process of growing up and breaking away made this more problematic for her. Her mother describes her as her "best" daughter and likes to take her shopping and to lunch with her friends. She remembers with fondness long years of helping Jessie fix her hair or study for school. She sometimes remarks that she wishes her daughter were a child again—when Jessie needed her more.

Descriptions of the "typical" anorexic family may or may not be true of most families with an anorexic member. If they are true, these patterns may either contribute to the disorder or be its effects. Parents and other family members, who invariably feel guilty and responsible, must not allow themselves to become paralyzed by these feelings. Instead—because their daughter's life could be in danger—parents must seek help for her, become involved in treatment, and be willing to change.

Don't Wait to Help!

Sharon, 5'8", lost fifty pounds, down from her high of 160, before her family noticed there was a problem. She was shocked by their extreme concern. "How can they be right? I look so fat," she said, as she took to wearing long-sleeved shirts, even in the summer, to hide her "fat" arms. When her parents, in desperation, referred her to the family doctor, she put weights in her pockets so that she would not weigh so little and "upset him needlessly."

When a parent or friend notices that a young woman has lost an extreme amount of weight, the anorexic should be confronted and referred immediately to a medical doctor, psychologist, or psychiatrist who is experienced with the disorder. One's natural response is to wait. "I don't want to overreact," "Maybe I'm wrong," "Maybe it'll go away"—all are typical rationales. For safety's sake, don't wait! Rapid weight loss of this magnitude is life-threatening. It is unlikely that the anorexic will begin to eat normally without help, and if she should, rapid weight gain and dramatic changes in diet are equally dangerous.

The treatment of anorexia nervosa requires several approaches, including: (1) behavior modification techniques, nutritional information, and possibly hospitalization and drug treatment to counter the starvation process; (2) individual psychotherapy to increase self-esteem and a sense of self-control; and (3) family therapy to help the family understand the anorexic and support her progress.

Medical treatment: stopping the starvation. Anorexia, like bulimia, is associated with a host of medical problems, many of which are the results of malnutrition and starvation, and anorexics may die unexpectedly at any time as a result of these complications. Anorexics have extreme sensitivity to cold (hypothermia), irregular heart rates (bradycardia), growth of extra fine body hair (lanugo), metabolic disturbance, and constipation. They lose calcium deposits in their bones and disrupt their electrolyte balance, the finely tuned ratio of nutrients and fluids in their system. Singer Karen Carpenter, who suffered from anorexia nervosa, died of heart failure as a result of potassium depletion. If the anorexic is also a habitual vomiter, she may experience the same problems as bulimics: tooth erosion, swelling in the parotid glands on each side of the face, gastrointestinal problems, and ulcers. She may have a short attention span and poor memory. Not surprisingly, the longer term the disorder, the more major the physical problems.

An anorexic who has lost a great deal of weight usually must be hospitalized to facilitate safe weight gain. Patients are required to eat balanced meals and watched carefully after eating to prevent vomiting. They usually must participate in peer, individual, and family therapy. Drugs may be prescribed, usually to treat the depression which often accompanies anorexia. Patients leave the hospital once their weight has stabilized.

Hospitalization is frightening to patients, and patients may resist the weight gain necessary to keep them alive. In *Kessa*, the girl decides: "She couldn't go to a hospital. She just couldn't! They'd stick tubes in her and all those thousands of calories would pour in and she'd swell up and get so fat she'd look like a blimp and just float away—" [6] Force feeding is not a common treatment, however, as patients generally begin eating upon entering the hospital.

Behavior modification techniques are useful in encouraging weight gain in hospital settings. These techniques are designed to help the patient, who is starving herself as a means of having control over her life, come to see eating as a positive, social experience, rather than something to be avoided. Behavior management techniques may also trigger significant anxieties about gaining weight. Some patients become terrified and insist on losing weight as soon as they leave the hospital. Others fear they will be unable to control their weight gain, becoming obese and/or bulimic. To address these fears and avoid chaotic eating patterns, behavior therapy should be combined with insight-oriented and familial approaches.

Individual psychotherapy: addressing the false perceptions. The therapist needs to appropriately confront an anorexic with the facts of her disorder, particularly its effects on her physiology. The therapist can help her become aware of and strengthen her sense of self by imagery, working with clay, and making collages. He or she will encourage the anorexic to care for herself by helping her to identify and express her feelings, to decide when to take care of others and when her needs come first, to find space (a room, a special time of day) where she is safe and alone. As her sense of self is strengthened, her autonomy, decision-making ability, and confidence in the validity of her own needs and feelings should also increase. At the same time, her thought distortions ("If I'm too fat, no one will love me" or "I've been bad and have to punish myself by not eating") need to be addressed.[7] Body imaging techniques can help her become more realistic about her body size. Participation in groups, more difficult for bulimics (who admit their problem) than anorexics (who often try to deny it), can sometimes be helpful in clarifying misperceptions of reality.

Family therapy: help for those who care about the anorexic. Most clinicians experienced with anorexia will ask family members of anorexics still living at home to meet with them regularly. Anorexia affects the entire family and family members find they need help dealing with the anorexic daughter. Treatment is most effective when family members are willing to support the therapist's decisions as to how best to work with the daughter in the context of the family.

Exercise: What Can Families Do?

If you suspect that your daughter or someone you know is anorexic, please consider these suggestions.

Refer her. The disorder is not treatable by family members, and adequate treatment may determine the child's survival. It is most preferable that she see a Christian therapist who has experience with the disorder. If none is available, because the disorder is difficult to treat, even by specialists, it is better that she see a non-Christian experienced with the disorder. Do not undercut the recommendations of these specialists.

Accept the diagnosis. Once the diagnosis is made by trained persons, do not take it personally, and do not label it as sin. Do realize that she needs special care at this time.

Support her. Express honest affection for her and be warmly supportive of her efforts. Talk with her about issues other than weight. As treatment progresses, setbacks are common.

Be optimistic about her progress and accept setbacks as a normal part of her treatment.

Avoid power struggles. Do not demand weight gain. Trust that good professionals can help her better than her parents can.

Protect her. Take responsibility off her shoulders. Do not allow her to shop and/or cook for the whole family.

Encourage her independence. Expect her to have her own opinions, ask her likes and dislikes, and respect these as much as possible.

Pray for her. An anorexic can be hard to love. But remember, she too is struggling to understand herself and her needs, and needs prayer.

"Just Take Me Home": Christians and Anorexia

Heavenly Father,

I have no idea where I am going. As my weight drops down, my life trickles away. How I long to die and be with you. . . . Let me see hope that things will get better. I know what I am doing cannot be within your will but I am unable to stop. Now that I am eighty-one pounds, I want to keep dieting until I die. I know food will not satisfy the hungers I have—for affection, confidence, job satisfaction, male attention, motherhood. Since food cannot substitute for these things, why bother with it at all? Just take me home. With the disobedience I am now wallowing in, I do not even know where that would be.

Christians too are vulnerable to anorexia nervosa, as this entry from a prayer journal documents. Christians with anorexia may manipulate their faith to justify their restrictive eating. To shun pride, to develop self-control, to be obedient: all become commands God has given them especially for their eating. They marshal Bible verses to identify their struggle to be thin with being humble ("Pride goeth before a fall") and with fighting Satan ("Stand fast therefore . . ."). Because the language is biblical, it is difficult to recognize this misuse of Scripture. Many anorexics secretly feel righteous, morally superior to their peers. Identifying that pride can be a step toward healing.

Do not call anorexia sin, label the sufferer a sinner or exhort her to "let go and let God" heal her and help her gain weight. There are no easy guides for helping Christian women who are anorexic separate their disorder from their faith. They will benefit, however, from asking for God's help in their struggle toward wholistic eating as they learn to recognize their starvation and to begin to identify the reasons they choose not to eat. Christians with anorexia can seek help, admitting their own need. They can make a conscious choice to become effective in a whole-life way, recognizing their own weakness and acknowledging the strength of God.

Anorexia is a complex disorder that cannot be treated by the individual, the family, or most pastors. Specialists, with the help of caring friends and family, are required to address the anorexic's medical and emotional needs and to help her find healthy, biblical alternatives to dieting as her defense against a frightening and unbearable reality. Girls who suffer from anorexia can escape from their "golden cage," their prison of conformity, and allow their eating and all their lives to become a glory to God.

5.

Transforming Our Eating Habits

Tanya worked hard at dieting and kept a 1000-calorie limit on her eating every day. She knew that for breakfast she would have a small bowl of cereal, a cup of skim milk, and one banana; at lunch she would have a salad with vinegar; at dinner she would have one slice of meat and a hot vegetable. Nothing ever changed, except that once every two weeks, no matter what she tried to prevent it, she would gorge herself for an evening . . . eating absolutely anything she wanted. All evening she loved it, but at the end of the evening, she would hate herself. As penance, she would pledge to start back on an even tougher diet tomorrow.

Anorexia and bulimia are only the most extreme manifestations of the national obsession with dieting. At any given time, the majority of American women are dieting. Or thinking they should. We rejoice with Oprah Winfrey when she shows off her new body in size-ten jeans—and when she regains much of the lost weight, the news is splashed all over the supermarket tabloids. We make fun of Elizabeth Taylor for not being able to keep it off, and cluck-cluck when our favorite news anchor gains weight, until everyone sighs in relief, "Oh, she's pregnant." At any given time, the best-seller list includes at least one diet book.

Rare is the woman who has not been on a diet. Dieting has become the norm in America, so much so that the "normal" woman diets and apologizes (whether she is thin or fat) if she is not on a diet.[1] One body size and shape become the ideal, and any other body shape is considered abnormal.

"I Start Feeling Trapped"

Dieting women will lose, and regain, literally hundreds of pounds over the course of a lifetime. About ten percent of those who go on diets actually keep the weight off permanently. Failure is built into most weight-loss regimes. Why don't diets work? They don't work because they force dieters to go against their own physiology, to deprive themselves, to live with guilt. They are based on negative imperatives ("don't eat this") rather than positive choices ("here is the way to health").

Most basically, dieting is based on fear of food. Food is bad; to eat it makes a person bad. When we diet, the decision about eating is made by the diet book or by some other arbitrary rule, rather than by our own internal hunger needs. We become a victim of the "magic number syndrome," in which we must weigh a certain weight or take in no more than a certain number of calories to feel good about ourselves. An older "prayer" from a Dear Abby column captures how ridiculous this can become. While this is obviously not a real prayer, it typifies the too-common longing among Christian women to deny themselves food, to feel pain, and to experience deprivation.

Calorie Counter's Prayer

The Lord is my shepherd; I shall not want,
He maketh me to lie down and do push-ups.
He giveth me Hollywood Bread.
He restoreth my waistline.
He leadeth me past the refrigerator for mine own sake.
He maketh me to partake of the green beans instead of the
*   potatoes.*
He leadeth me past the pizzeria.
Yea though I walk through the bakery,

I shall not falter, for thou art with me.
Thy Tab and Fresca, they comfort me.
Thou preparest a diet for me in the presence of mine enemies.
Thou anointest my lettuce with low-cal oil.
My cup will not overflow.
Surely RyKrisp and D-Zerta shall follow me all the days of my
*   life,*
And I will dwell with pangs of hunger forever.

AMEN

Who can live like that for very long? Who can eat like that for more than a few weeks? Most women can't. Dieting causes feelings of being trapped—the psychological term is "cognitive claustrophobia"—and self-deprivation. Carol describes the dilemma this way: "I feel like I need someone to take care of me and yet I cannot even take care of myself by eating an extra egg. I start feeling more and more trapped . . . needy . . . desperate." Most explode into a binge sooner or later. To put a particular food off-limits brings out cravings for that food. If you don't allow yourself to eat that M&M chocolate candy that has been offered to you, you are likely to crave a piece of chocolate cake—the richer the better. Sooner or later, you get that chocolate you wanted—lots and lots of it—far more than you really craved and more than you would have eaten if you had taken that M&M. You can trust your body to guide your eating more than you can trust a diet.

Dieting, then, creates "forbidden" foods, which have the lure of sin and, once tasted, seduce us into wanting more. Most dieters have an imaginary line in their minds, dividing what is permissible from what is off-limits on their diet. If anything happens to make them cross that line, they excessively overeat, sometimes bingeing. Psychologists have used "counter regulation" studies to demonstrate this.[2] Dieters and non-dieters are paid to participate in what they are told is a taste test of a new product, typically something like ice cream. They are assured that they can eat whatever amount they need to establish the taste preference. Before the taste test, they are given some forbidden food, perhaps a brownie, to "clear the palate" for the taste test. When they begin the test, the dieters are much more likely than the non-dieters to overeat when given the chance. Once they are forced off their diet by a brownie, they seem to tell themselves that it doesn't matter what they eat now that they have blown their diet. They might as well eat a lot while they are at it. Tomorrow it's back to the celery. Their only measure of acceptable eating is what is on their list. They have never learned to pay attention to their internal cues for eating.

Exercise:
Legalizing
Forbidden
Foods

1. Make a list of favorite foods that you would not eat because they are outrageously rich or likely to trigger a binge. Choose a target food from this list, one that seems less threatening to try.

2. Visualize yourself looking at this food. Why does it frighten you? Why is it bad? Confront the fear by practicing looking at and touching the food item without eating it.

3. Visualize yourself eating the food. Are you afraid you cannot stop? What makes you want to keep eating? What strategies would help you stop? A friend, perhaps? Another activity planned? Limiting the amount of food available?

4. When the anxiety has decreased, develop a plan to taste other food items, one each week—a little bit every time you want it. Serve yourself a little, and use your strategies for stopping eating. Put the rest away or throw it away if you must to stop yourself from eating.

5. If you eat more than you'd like, address your awareness directly. Recognize that you are eating in response to mouth hunger. Name it BINGE with every bite you take. This awareness should slow you down enough to move the food item out of reach. If not, reevaluate your starting and stopping strategies and try it again next week. One you have eaten in moderation, congratulate yourself, then figure out what made the experience successful.

Why Does Dieting Cause Overeating?

Why does dieting actually make us want to eat *more*? The answer is rooted in our physiology.[3] As we stop eating, our body decides that we might starve to death and tries to protect us. Our brain increases the demands of our appetite, so that we want to eat more. Our body also decreases its metabolism (the rate at which we use up calories for energy) to conserve strength. As a result, over time, we have to diet more strenuously to use up the same amount of calories as before. Eventually we binge, use up those binge calories more slowly, and gain weight. We then decide we need to go on a stricter diet. Soon we are caught in a physically dangerous cycle of undereating and overeating, of losing weight and gaining weight. This "yo-yo" syndrome is more stressful for our bodies than being fat and may contribute to the health problems that occur in overweight people with chaotic eating histories.

Dieting fights the body's natural "set point," or preferred metabolic rate and body fat proportion.[4] We all know some thin people who could daily eat three three-course meals without gaining an ounce, and others who claim they gain weight by smelling a rich dessert. When our weight is below a certain set point, our bodies perceive themselves as starving and push us to eat more. When our weight is above that point, our bodies modulate hunger and metabolize food less efficiently. Regardless of our dieting and exercising, our bodies fight to be at a certain weight. Research suggests that repetitively gaining and losing weight may, over the long term, change an individual's set point to a *higher* level—so that every time we regain weight, we gain a little more.

For some women, chaotic eating destabilizes the normal hormonal cycle and metabolic patterns underlying sexuality, leading to irregular periods or even the cessation of menstruation. Sexual responsivity may become erratic, with women developing either depressed sexual arousal or impulsive, heightened sexual drives.

Dieting can never give us what we really want. The anorexic girl believes that dieting will bring her to a state of physical perfection and attractiveness. Instead, it turns her into a scarecrow figure who can only think about food. For most of us, dieting makes us feel like failures. Most women can sometimes follow a diet, but find it harder and harder to maintain weight loss as our bodies continually struggle to regain equilibrium. As a result, a woman blames herself for what is a biological phenomenon: her body sabotages dieting to prevent starvation and struggles to stabilize itself at a biologically programmed weight that may be somewhat higher than she prefers. And she feels like a loser!

If Not Dieting, What?

If we don't diet, how do we decide what is appropriate to eat? We have to learn to *think about what we eat*—in response to our body's needs. We need to discover what it feels like to be hungry; then react reasonably to that physiological hunger.

Stopping dieting does not mean we throw caution to the wind, eating whatever we want whenever we want. It means we spend time thinking about what and how we want to eat, rather than what we are not going to eat and then drooling over what we'd like to have. We need to eat in a thoughtful, planned, conscious, disciplined manner according to our own personal tastes and appetite.

It's a tough transition. First you have to identify your hunger and then explore what will satisfy that hunger. In her book *Breaking Free from Compulsive Eating*, Geneen Roth describes her struggle to overcome compulsive eating by giving up dieting.[5] When she first decided that she would eat whatever her body wanted, her body craved chocolate chip cookies. For dinner that first day she baked chocolate chip cookies and ate as many as she wanted, savoring each one. That made her full. She stopped eating. The next day, when she asked her body what it wanted, visions of raw chocolate chip dough floated into her head, so she had three lumps of raw dough and two chocolate chip cookies. That made her full. Then for two weeks she ate chocolate chip cookies for breakfast, lunch, dinner, and snack, and after the fifteenth day, she never wanted to look at another chocolate chip cookie again. It was no longer forbidden her and she did not crave it in a compulsive way. She was learning to listen to her body and to trust her body to take care of her needs. While she chose a dramatic way to overcome her fear of food, most of us would find a more gradual tuning in to hunger a more effective way to overcome fear of food.

Exercise: Learning to Experience and Satisfy Hunger

This exercise is designed to help you become aware of the internal, physiological processes secondary to eating and to help you recognize your specific hungers for foods. Write down some of your thoughts to help you recall your feelings and sensations later.

1. Let yourself get hungry. Locate the feelings of hunger in your body. Where do you feel hungry? How does your stomach feel? Do you feel shaky, hollow, tense? What is happening in your mouth, your chest, your legs? What noises can you hear?

2. Visualize the hunger. What form has it taken? Is it a black glob or a roaring lion or a giant mouth? What emotion is the hunger expressing? Identify your physical hunger as separate and different from an emotional hunger.

3. Now identify what your hunger is calling for. What would satisfy the hunger that you feel?

Allow yourself to visualize all sorts of food, even forbidden foods. Which food would you choose to eat? Why? What qualities make this food appealing? Color? Texture? Smell? Do you have strong memories attached to this food? Are those memories of physical or emotional hungers that were satisfied or problematic for you?

4. Take a bite of the food you desire. Put your fork down and evaluate the experience. Savor that piece of food.

How does it feel in your mouth? Where can you taste it? Identify the textures, the taste, the location in your mouth that is satisfying. As you swallow it, trace how and where it is going. What does it do to your sensation of hunger? How appealing is it now? What makes it so?

5. Continue to eat until your hunger is gone. After each bite, put your fork down and ask yourself the same questions as for the first. How did your physical sensation of hunger change? What happened to your image of the hunger? What emotion is it expressing now? How does it feel to be satisfied?

Identify how your stomach, your mouth, your chest, your legs feel now.

Did you eat beyond the point of satisfaction? How can you tell? What physical signs can you note? What emotional sensations? What emotions may confuse your ability to attend to your physical messages about your need to start and stop eating?

When I have used the hunger exercise with groups, participants have been startled by their findings. One woman recognized that what was most satisfying to her hunger was a variety of tastes and textures in small portions: a dab of tuna, a few olives, some crispy salty crackers, a radish, some malted milk balls. She began designing more interesting, diverse, smaller meals for herself and really tasting her food. Another woman found that eating something delicious about one hour before her scheduled meal made her more sensitive to her cues of fullness and less fearful of succumbing to mouth hunger.

All the women found it difficult to "hear" their signals of fullness—the sign that they should stop eating. So we explored different signals. First, we gave up all typical signs that it's time to stop eating: the plate is empty, other people have finished, the bag is empty, we've consumed enough calories. Then we experimented with obviously overfilling our plates and not emptying them, then underfilling them and pausing before we got more food, then eating alone, then eating only with others agreeing to observe, then eating fast versus eating slowly, then eating single types of food versus varieties, then snacking at the first sign of hunger versus waiting until we were starving. This experimental, self-aware approach helped each woman identify factors that affected her own personal awareness of satiety.

When you are beginning to change your diet mentality, start by eating food in a less circumscribed, restrictive manner, as outlined by the exercises "Legalizing Forbidden Foods" and "Learning to Experience and Satisfy Hunger." Eat a wider variety of foods, including forbidden foods, adding one or two at a time. Feel free to eat regularly or frequently during the day but eat in proportion to your hunger. Don't eat more than your body tells you it needs. Although you may at first eat in bizarre or unpredictable ways, your eating should soon settle and you should enjoy and feel comfortable about eating what your body wants when it wants it. Most people do not gain excessive amounts of weight as a result of developing an appropriate hunger response. Rather, their weight stabilizes, on the average, at a weight that's reasonable for them. Their eating has, however, become freer and more satisfying as a result.

Tanya, the woman with the rigid diet described at the beginning of this chapter, went through a slow, careful process of weaning herself away from her diet in order to eat by a different guide, her body. She began to introduce variation in her diet. She let herself daily eat something that she wanted just because it tasted good. Eventually Tanya's eating became freer and less constrained by external standards and, at the same time, more consistent with what she thought healthy eating should be. Her binges became less regular as she became less rigid in her eating. Through much of the process, especially at first, Tanya was terrified that she would rebound and gain a great deal of weight. The process of transition took place over a six-month period, slow enough to allow her body's metabolism to stabilize at a more reasonable level. She had learned successfully how to eat in response to her hunger.

How Are You Eating Right Now?

In order to face the facts about our eating problems, we need to know what the facts are. We may have a vague sense that we eat too much, or the wrong things, or at the wrong times, without knowing what our eating is really like. The first critical factor in understanding our eating problem is to get as specific as possible about how and when and why we eat in a way that does not satisfy us. Document your pattern of eating, using the format on the following page.

Write daily and in detail, recording what you ate, whether you felt it was a binge, all the circumstances of the eating (where, when, with whom, slow or fast, etc.), what emotions you felt, what thoughts you had, and as many other details as are important for you. Pay more attention to why and how you eat than what you eat. Do not use this to count calories. After two weeks, you will have objective information by which to highlight major problem points and to measure your progress. What are your triggers to overeating? When you get down to the details about your eating, some patterns become obvious. When you understand specifically what factors affect your eating, you can manage better the circumstances that affect inappropriate eating.

Journal of Eating Experiences

When:	3 P.M.	5:30 P.M.
Where:	In the pantry	Dinner table with family
Food eaten:	Three handfuls of salted almonds	Salad Lambchop
Feelings before eating:	I wish I'd stayed for church coffee hour . . . regret.	Tense about family liking the food I prepared.
Thoughts after eating:	I am ashamed of hiding here eating.	I was so busy watching them, I never noticed what I ate.
Was the eating satisfying?	Yes, at the beginning.	I didn't notice the taste of my food.
Level of hunger before/after: 0 to 10	3 – definite hunger 8 – full	5 – not hungry 10 – way over full
What have I learned?	I could have eaten a few and been satisfied.	Pay attention to my own eating experience.
What could I do differently?	Don't eat in pantry. Plan to stay for coffee hour.	Join my family but don't eat unless hungry.

Andrea documented her eating in this way and began to realize she had several "trouble spots" in her day:

Andrea gets up every morning just in time to dress and rush to work. She eats breakfast on the way there, usually a muffin purchased at the grocery store when she does the family's weekly shopping. Once at work, she answers the telephone and files papers all day, not even stopping for lunch, because her boss wants someone to cover the telephone during lunch hour, while everyone else is away. Instead, she usually snacks during the day. By five, Andrea is exhausted and hungry. She stops by the store on the way home for two Snickers bars and eats them before she walks in the house. She knows that, once she comes home, she'll have to fix dinner for two teenagers and her husband, and it seems that lately one or another of them does not come home for dinner. So she prepares dinner, nibbling as she works, and sits down in front of the television, still nibbling, to wait until someone gets home to eat with her.

When Andrea realized the pattern she had established, she began getting up earlier, in time to take a long walk every morning and to eat a healthier breakfast before going to work. She began preparing lunch, making it more interesting, and planned a late afternoon snack. She volunteered at a local hospice after work and made arrangements with her family to take care of their own dinners unless they let her know their plans earlier. When she began to take control of her own eating, she found that eating improved and she felt more satisfied with work and home life.

Women often go wrong in their eating when they are responsible for feeding other people. We can become overinvested in creating food and making others eat. And when they don't eat, we may experience disappointment that pushes us back to food, even when we are not hungry. Women's constant accessibility to food complicates their avoidance of overeating.

Sharon feels great. She had black coffee and grapefruit after she got the kids off to school. She cleaned house all morning, then ate a satisfying tuna sandwich for lunch. Now she is planning the family's evening meal, making sure it is healthy and well balanced. She realizes that she needs to go to the supermarket to pick up the mozzarella for the casserole. Once in the market she sees some freshly baked rolls that would go great with dinner and some eclairs that her husband really enjoys. Driving home in the car, she decides to taste the eclairs. So, she eats four eclairs, one right after the other, only too late recognizing that her morning of appropriate eating has given way to a disastrous afternoon.

In this vignette there are cues that help Sharon identify her "trouble spots" for her eating. For instance, if she eats while she is driving, she is likely to lose track of why she is eating. Eating while doing something else, like driving, studying, or cooking, is a common trigger for eating inappropriately. It is important to concentrate on our eating. Sharon may have been hungry or craving chocolate and bought the eclairs as a result. If so, she should decide that she will freely give herself an eclair and allow herself to sit down and enjoy it. If she savors this eclair, purposefully and consciously, she is less likely to be caught in the trap of eating too much without even thinking about it.

Often the process of monitoring how and why we eat will bring an improvement to our eating behavior. So much of our eating is inadvertent; we eat without thinking until it is too late. This process of documentation forces us to think about our eating, particularly if we review our records with someone else. For some of us, this writing format may take a great deal of discipline to maintain. But when we pay attention to our eating and choose to eat what we think will taste good at that very moment, we are less likely to overeat or to feel guilty after eating.

After a week of food monitoring in your journal, go back

and identify what alternative choices or actions would have enabled you to escape your episodes of wrong eating. Typical alternatives include talking to someone, leaving the context that encourages eating, preparing something more healthy and satisfying, rewarding yourself with a favorite activity, taking a walk outside, cooking a new recipe, writing in your journal, praying. Write down whatever you decide would have helped in a list that you keep handy. The next time that you find yourself in a similar situation, or with similar feelings or thoughts, consult your list. Act on one of the choices; do not try to clench your teeth and wait it through. Change your mode of response.

You Can Eat in a Healthy Way

In our helter-skelter world, too many of us seem to eat poorly either because we have too much to do and feel we have little time for healthful eating, or because we have too little to do so we feel compelled to eat to quell our emotions. Good nutrition need not take a great deal of time, but it can be satisfying and rewarding.

Good nutrition begins with the four basic food groups: meat or meat substitutes, fruits and vegetables, milk and milk products, and grains. A balanced intake provides you the energy you need to function.

Too often we have a candy bar, deciding to stint on dinner later to compensate for the calories. A candy bar is no substitute for steamed vegetables. Rich foods make one less healthy and capable, as Daniel braved the king's wrath to prove (Daniel 1). You metabolize food better, feel better, and look better if you first meet your needs for adequate nutrition—and you are less likely to get that candy bar from the machine during your afternoon break if your body's basic needs are met.

Good nutrition is not boring. Sometimes we are too focused on what we *cannot* eat, or we get into "eating ruts." Monday night is spaghetti night; Tuesday night is chicken and broccoli; Wednesday night is sandwiches; and so it goes. Or perhaps we allow ourselves to eat only salad and fruits every meal.

A basic rule for healthful, satisfying eating is variety. You should be experimenting with foods and enjoying the variety of different tastes, textures, and colors. Many families maximize their use of seasonal foods because they introduce enjoyable variety: homemade bread and heavy soups in winter, summer fruits and vegetables, fall squashes and potatoes, and New Year's Day black-eyed peas and hog jowl.

If you keep a record of your eating and discover that you have little variety, begin introducing more diverse foods in your diet. Try fresh peas, quiche, or fresh fruit salad. A limited eating repertoire may seem difficult to break. Rigidity represents safety. Yet, by moving outside the tight circle of familiar foods, you can begin to identify and trust your tastes and find that healthful eating is as rewarding in its own way as eating that "forbidden" candy bar.

Foods that are closest to their natural state are generally more varied and interesting, and more healthful for you. Avoid too much saturated fat, additives, preservatives, cholesterol, sodium, and sugar. Eat foods with adequate starch and fiber. Most Americans consume too much protein. A diet with more complex carbohydrates—grains, rice, beans—and less meat is now recommended by the American Dietary Association, American Heart Association, and American Cancer Society, among other groups, as the most healthful for us to eat. *Jane Brody's Good Food Book: Living the High-Carbohydrate Way* presents these ideas clearly and backs them up with recipes for family or individual use.[6]

Although more healthful foods may take longer to cook, most of us have a labor-saving microwave or pressure cooker, or with a little planning on Saturday morning, can prepare some healthy options for later in the week. I grew up in a family in which both mom and dad worked. Saturday mornings, we three kids took turns cooking a salad, main dish, and dessert, under mom's supervision. I enjoyed those mornings (my sister and I still tease my brother for being so slow), learned many recipes (and how they taste at every stage in the preparation), and still prefer to have someone in the kitchen with me while I work.

Eating should be an event that is accepted, even honored, by giving it fair time and careful attention. Being conscious about eating and all the circumstances surrounding mealtimes will decrease thoughtless eating. The "Make Eating a Celebration" exercise offers the opportunity to reevaluate what factors enrich an eating experience. Don't transfer traditions or recommendations wholesale or directly. Tailor them to your own set of circumstances; devise new rituals; keep changing mealtime patterns. One woman, in carrying out this exercise, realized that she had put off buying new china, assuming that she would soon get a roommate or maybe get married, because she felt that she, eating alone, wasn't worthy of fine china. Another woman loved planning interesting, healthful meals to eat by candlelight and charmed her friends by inviting them over now and again to share in her pleasure.

Exercise:
Make
Eating a
Celebration

1. Visualize your present eating arrangement. What are meals like for you in your home? Who does the cooking? How do you feel about that? If you live alone, how do you feel about eating alone?

What do mealtimes mean to you? Are they social occasions? Good times? Unpredictable? Lonely? Upsetting?

What about the meal gives you pleasure? Discomfort?

2. Visualize how you wish your meals would be. Do you eat off good plates, or save those for guests? Do you eat in a pleasant location? Do you eat the same foods over and over, never planning what to eat or shopping ahead for a special dinner?

3. How can you make eating more of a celebration that makes you feel special? Can you develop a ritual for beginning or ending a meal?

You Can Move in a Healthy Way

For many women, vigorous movement is crucial for developing self-esteem and body awareness. Moderate aerobic exercise improves one's sense of self, increases the efficiency of one's metabolism, and can influence set point. Little boys learn sports, but little girls too often are encouraged to keep themselves pretty, neat, clean. By not encouraging girls to be physically active, we estrange women from their bodies. We encourage their ignorance of body cues, their passivity, their sense of incompetence.

> *Vicki, at twenty-five, felt she had tried every diet without success and still counted every calorie she ate. A quiet, self-effacing woman, she felt trapped by her weight and frustrated by a stressful job that was more isolating than she wanted. When asked to journal her experiences, she recorded every morsel of food she ate but found it difficult to talk of needs and feelings. She decided to start jogging, a mile at a time, three times a week. She found to her surprise that she really enjoyed the feeling of movement: its freedom, its feeling of being in charge of her body, of having no constraints on her body, attention, or time. Her enthusiasm and her sense of achievement became the impetus for increasing her sense of self-esteem, her control in her life. She eventually was able to mobilize herself to ask for a revised job description and modify her job to better meet her needs. She was surprised to realize that she had not worried about weight for months.*

To help you modify wrong eating, consider adding regular vigorous movement to your lifestyle or changing your present level of physical activity. Choose an activity you enjoy, preferably an aerobic one that you can do regularly—walking, jogging, swimming, rowing, racquetball, dance. Movement should not be extreme or become addictive, an alternative path to the perfect body, as the modern fitness craze tends to encourage. Integrate physical activity into your daily schedule. Take the extra time to walk between shopping errands rather than drive. Use stairs instead of an escalator or elevator. Do your cleaning, food preparation, and yard work by hand. When possible, stand up or stretch now and again at your work site. Rescue the children from Nintendo and take them out sledding, hiking, or playing ball. Many women find that vigorous movement, when practiced appropriately, helps improve self-esteem, effectively counteracts depression, and provides the stimulant they need for recognizing their active control in their eating life.

Toward Transformation

The approach we advocate may seem like a slow, difficult way to control eating problems, but there are no quick solutions. Any bookstore has shelves of fad diet books, or surgery may seem like an easy answer, but these techniques have been shown to be ineffective and often dangerous. For the problem eater, to eat in a more self-aware way is to begin the process of changing eating habits, a process that can demonstrate in a dramatic, daily way that God can transform our eating and our lives in powerful ways.

6. *Filling the Empty Spaces*

I was a thin child who began to eat away isolation after school in an empty house. I didn't get fat until the birth of my second child; it was a time of poor marriage relations. I couldn't face the conflicts and turmoil while pregnant. Repeatedly over the years my "fat times" have occurred when problems were overwhelming and I had little control.
— Sandra, age thirty-six

Too often we eat to fill an empty space—to feed an emotional hunger. We eat when we're lonely. We eat when we're depressed. We eat when we're angry. Or bored. Or anxious. Then we feel stuffed and in an emotional fog, but at least the hurt has gone away—for a while. Food anesthetizes the pain, but it doesn't make it go away. As Susie Orbach writes, "Food cannot make things better, it cannot fill up whatever emptiness there is inside."[1]

I Eat When I'm Bored

We all do it sometimes: idly snack, restlessly peer into the refrigerator, unthinkingly grab a cookie out of the jar. We're bored, so we eat. However, if we do this *habitually* , we need to evaluate how we spend our time—which should be filled with satisfying activity, not food.

Sensations of physical emptiness may also reflect emptiness in relationships. For women, relationships are primary, life-giving sources. When a woman says she is bored, what she often really means is, "I'm lonely."

Doreen is a competent musician and an attractive woman. She graduated from college with a degree in music performance and enjoys playing at her friends' weddings and for church performances and concerts. Yet she struggles with relationships with her three roommates who, she feels, are more socially adept and attractive than she. When she comes home from work, her roommates usually have friends over. She feels awkward then, as if she has no right to be there, and, even if she has not had dinner, slinks to her room to stay until they leave. By then, she is so hungry and feels so inept that she raids the kitchen, eating whatever her roommates have in the refrigerator and finishing off all the cookies and chips in the cupboard.

On a college campus on Friday and Saturday nights, groups of girls are likely to binge as a group. Girls might "do anorexia" at other times, choosing to fast as a group, holding pep sessions and sharing ideas for minimizing the dizziness or cravings for food. This group gorging or group fasting provides a temporary sense of emotional connectedness. But it doesn't remove the loneliness.

Anne was a shy college senior who couldn't understand why God had not brought her husband-to-be into her life. She knew her compulsive binges were related to her feelings of loneliness and fears of being alone forever, but she could not stop herself from overeating. In the course of counseling, Anne decided to assume a more active role in initiating conversations with others at college, in joining groups of students doing fun things, and in attending church functions she thought she might enjoy. She gradually became less focused on her emotional deficits and fears, which made it easier to establish good relationships with men as well as women. Her eating became more consistent, and she was less obsessed with finding a man and more fun for others to be around.

Women know that food is not a good answer to loneliness, but it seems a lot easier than making the effort to develop relationships. But it is possible—indeed, absolutely necessary—to stop hiding behind food and reach out to others, as Anne found out. Women who nurture all sorts of relationships—friendships with women, with men, with children, with older people—find little room for boredom in their lives.

I Eat When I Feel Down

Depression among women is as prevalent as the common cold. A chronic, low-grade depression may rob a person of the energy to deal effectively with her eating choices. Women often carry around a vague sense of depression, of not being "good enough" as a mother or wife or Christian. We blame ourselves for this and feel dissatisfied, but we are not quite sure what we can do about it. It is easier and more soothing to nibble on leftover Christmas candy canes—or your child's dinner—than to do something more active to beat the blues.

Why are women depressed more often than men? There are many reasons, but one factor is that our society values individualism and success more than it values caring for other people, especially children. The things that women do well and often spend a lot of time doing—feeding people, taking care of children, fostering relationships, taking care of the weak and the vulnerable—are little valued in our society. We are willing to pay a plumber about five times what we are willing to pay someone who takes care of our children. Those qualities that are encouraged in women more than men—empathy, intuition, dependability, ability to cooperate, and warmth—go unrewarded.[2] For Christians, of course, these are Christlike qualities. But even in our Christian community, spiritual caregiving is often undervalued.

Eating masks other feelings. After overeating, it is easier to get angry at the food or at oneself than it is to face the feelings of worthlessness. But the self-critical feelings soon return and are more intense because of the overeating episode.

Or perhaps when we are "successfully dieting" we use it to prove to ourselves that we are good enough to be loved. But the mask slips, we overeat, and each time we try to cover the feelings again, they become harder and harder to ignore.

At forty-five, Donna felt her life revolved around the kitchen and the supermarket. When the children were younger, she had enjoyed making them special breakfasts, surprise school lunches, and a family evening meal when the family had time to sit together and talk. But now her teenagers seemed to have little appreciation for fine meals. They wanted snacks and fast food. She was both hurt and angry about their insensitivity. Food delicacies became her solace, as she wandered around the house nibbling on gourmet tidbits, "feeling like a cast-off Reebok." In counseling we worked on defining who she was and what she cared about and how to develop her skills. Eventually she became deeply involved in the cause of world hunger and gave twenty hours a week as a volunteer to support a famine relief agency. Her obsession with food faded as she took responsibility for feeding others much more needy.

The best antidote to depression is *action*. Getting out of bed when you feel like sleeping in, trying out something new when the old rut would be more comfortable, making choices when you'd rather be passive—these actions counter depression. Battling food rather than depression is futile and subverts real healing.

For some people, mealtimes trigger childhood feelings of being small, helpless, and hopeless—the basic components of depression. These early experiences subconsciously contribute to distress about eating. The "Mealtime Memories" exercise may help you identify the deep-seated beliefs and feelings about eating that underlie your discomfort about food. One woman using this exercise noted that mealtimes were always tense because her father might start yelling, so she just gobbled her food and escaped to her room. It is no wonder that secret eating, especially potato chips in her bedroom, is the most satisfying eating for her. Another woman, retired and widowed, described mealtimes as the loneliest times of the day without her family nearby for sharing the day's events. This made eating unbearably sad for her and contributed to her pattern of eating nonnutritious snack food all day.

Exercise:
Mealtime
Memories

1. Imagine you are, as an adult, at a family dinner at your parents' home, with as many family members as possible.

How is everyone getting along? Are there conflicts or tensions between people? Does it feel good to be there?

Whom do you feel closest to? How are other people eating? How are you eating? Are you comfortable with your eating?

Visualize clearing the table. Who does it? Who doesn't? Who eats what is left over? What are your impulses about the leftover food?

2. Imagine you are much younger, about eight years old, and at mealtime with your family.

Did you all eat together, or take turns? What happened when meals began? Did you pray together then?

Who did the cooking? Did you wish something was different about your mother, or about your meals? Did you wish she would sit down more often? Did she eat with pleasure or pick at her food? Who served the food? Did you take your own, or did your parents put food on your plates? Who decided the size portion? Were you told to eat everything on your plate? What happened if you did not? How did you feel about that?

Did you look forward to mealtimes? What happened there besides eating? Storytelling? Shouting? Teasing? Punishment?

3. How do your childhood memories affect your adult mealtime patterns and preferences?

I Eat When I Feel Out of Control

Control is a key issue in all eating problems. Women on a diet delight in their control and hate themselves when they lose control. Women with bulimia may enjoy the feeling of losing control during a binge, but those sensations quickly give way to guilt and intensified efforts at self-control. The anorexic girl prides herself on maintaining perfect control. She does the impossible, although she may die for it, and we find ourselves envying her.

Why is control such a big issue for women? In our culture, and certainly within Christian circles, women often feel overpowered by men. In a marriage, the wife may feel unheard in negotiations for power, money, or shared household tasks. Mothers feel they must subordinate their needs to those of their children, often to the exclusion of their own needs. Feeling they have little control, but fearful of asserting their own needs, women find themselves trapped: They want what they decide they have no right to request. Other women have trouble knowing what they want and making decisions for themselves.

These feelings of lack of control carry over into eating, and women feel that food, too, controls them. Eating problems are blamed on others: "My husband loves pistachio ice cream and so I buy it. If he did not like it so much, it would not be around to tempt me." "My mother taught me to clean my plate." This attitude, however, is a trap. To eat, or not to eat, is a personal choice, an exercise of our will.

Anger may underlie a sense of helplessness and depression. We turn to food when we are frustrated. When we are fed up, we chow down. And the food dulls the anger, but it does not address the source of our anger. Anger is a powerful sign that something needs to change, and anger itself can energize positive change.[3] Stuffing our anger with food does not help us make the changes necessary to make our lives more satisfying.

I confess that I eat compulsively when I am angry, especially when I am angry at myself. During one of the thousands of rewrites of this manuscript, I was feeling very frustrated with myself for not figuring out how to structure one of the chapters in a clearer way. After pacing the floor and scolding myself for a few minutes, I became convinced that the barbecue-flavored potato chips would inspire me to better writing. I ate more handfuls than I care to admit, but when I calmed down, I could see the real problem more clearly. I was tired; I needed to take a break and do something else rather than keep banging my head against the proverbial wall. And, a few days later when I sat down again with the chapter, the solution came more easily to hand. In this situation, my desire to eat wrongly was the signal that I was not dealing effectively with a problem that made me feel angry.

Problem eaters may feel out of control, and use their eating in an effort to take control of their lives. Teenagers are quick to use eating—or not eating—as a weapon in their struggles with their parents.

> Kim started restricting her food intake at age twelve because she thought she was getting "paunchy with thighs that looked like Hubbard squash." She started skipping some meals and eating heartily at others. Her mother demanded that Kim eat healthily. Sometimes Kim ate "to get her mother off her back." At other times she exploded, "I can eat whatever I want. You cannot make me eat." As her mother put more pressure on her, full-family arguments ensued at the dinner table, and Kim retreated into secretive laxative abuse after dinner. Kim only began to modify her self-defeating, angry behavior when she realized she was hurting herself and hungering for real changes in her emotional life and relationships. Ultimately, she was the only one who could control her eating.

For healing of eating problems, recognize your sense of control, in eating and other areas of your life. For change to take place, acknowledge that eating is a personal choice. *I choose to put food in my mouth. I am the only one who can choose what, when, and how to eat. Food cannot control me. I control food.*

You may recognize your choice in starting to eat but find yourself asking, "Why can't I stop eating?" You are asking the wrong question. When you catch yourself eating wrongly, ask instead, "Why do I choose to eat now? What needs am I meeting? How can I more constructively meet those needs?" We are experienced in thinking of the limits to our control, instead of recognizing and using more judiciously the control we already have. But we will remain stuck in our present patterns unless we can acknowledge our choice in establishing and maintaining eating patterns.

Women who feel out of control in many areas of their lives often choose to exercise excessive control over their eating. The mother with three small children under five years of age, the housewife relocated cross-country for her husband's job, the student who struggles to do well and still makes poor grades— all know the experience of powerlessness. Rather than focusing on ways in which our control is limited, however, we need to recognize and enhance areas where we do have control. Join a mothers' group, start a visitors' group in the church, locate a tutor—in these ways, begin to address the areas of feeling powerless. Acknowledge that in other areas of life, you *do* have a great deal of control.

I Eat Because I've Been Hurt

Many women with eating problems have been sexually abused, among bulimics a shocking fifty-eight percent.[4] This rate is almost twice the thirty percent of American women who report sexual victimization during the school years. It is probably no coincidence that eating problems have risen dramatically just as reports of sexual abuse of children have increased.

Sexually abused children show four major long-term effects—and all four parallel emotional struggles common in women with eating problems.[5] Sexual abuse victims assume that those they trust will eventually *betray* them. Someone they counted on has hurt them, and they are uneasy to fully trust anyone again. *Traumatic sexualization*, the fact that the girl was introduced to sexual experiences at a too-young age, leaves a variety of emotional scars. The woman may be sensitized to touch, overreact to affection, be susceptible to repeated victimization, be afraid of sexuality, or behave in sexually inappropriate ways. *Stigmatization* occurs because the child feels dirty or guilty, even though she is not to blame for the victimization. This sense of "damaged goods" becomes internalized as chronic low self-esteem. *Disempowerment* is a sense of helplessness that develops because the child is unable to prevent or terminate the sexual contact. This feeling of not having control is heightened if protective action does not occur after the girl discloses the sexual actions.

Many women with eating disorders fit the profile of a survivor of childhood sexual abuse. They feel betrayed in relationships; they are unenthusiastic about sexuality; they reflect a chronically poor sense of self; they feel that nothing in life is under control. Perhaps they focus these issues onto eating struggles because it would be too painful to deal with their histories of victimization. Some women have blocked out these experiences.

> *Even though it was difficult initially for her to recall, as a child Marguerite was sexually abused repeatedly by her uncle. Now, as an adult, she finds herself unable to feel safe in a relationship unless she perceives herself as thinner than her boyfriend's old girlfriends. She has been caught in a web of destructive, addictive relationships to men. She is searching for the sense of well-being she feels in the initial romance of a new relationship. When the euphoria fades,*

she begins to obsess about her body, blaming it for undermining her boyfriend's attention and commitment to her.

For Marguerite nothing could change until she dealt with her past. Her understanding of herself as powerless and unlovable, set in motion by her sexual abuse experience, led her to seek out positive reflections in codependent relationships. Her challenge was in determining her own value from the inside out.

It is critical to find a counselor or support group to assist in recovery toward reclaiming control, love, and hope in oneself. Groups for incest survivors or Courage to Heal groups[6] can be found in most communities; a local mental health center or women's organization such as the YWCA can refer those interested in such groups.

Past sexual victimization does not absolve the survivor of personal responsibility in the present. Feeling helpless is not the same as *being* helpless. You can make choices. You do make decisions. You are in control of your life—and with God's guidance you can act responsibly in every decision you make— even in your eating.

Exercise:
Body
Imaging

1. Provide yourself modeling clay, a private space, ample time, and gentle background music.
2. Think of yourself as a little girl and remember the ways you felt at ease in your body. Model the clay into a form or shape that somehow depicts that feeling.
3. Think of yourself as an adolescent and recall your anxieties and pleasures as your body developed sexually. Model the clay into a form that depicts those adolescent feelings.
4. Think of yourself in your twenties or thirties, or pregnant, or as a new mother, or at some

other key developmental period of your life. Model your feelings about your body at that time.

5. Think of your body feelings now and model them into a form.

6. Ask these questions:

What do the various forms tell you about your changes in feelings?

Were there themes of sexual attractiveness or sexual fears that came up at any period?

Which forms elicit the strongest feelings? Were any of the forms unrealistically heavy or thin? Why?

Did the process of working with clay provide you a freeing sensual experience?

Toward True Healing

Eating cannot heal us. If we are emotionally hungry, food is not going to be satisfying. The emotional hunger must be addressed directly. We can find healing only within the context of our community of faith and in our innermost experience of our relationship to God. Our goal is spiritual wholeness.

Christians are called into loving, caring relationships with one another. It is not easy to negotiate mutually satisfying intimate relationships. As the codependent movement has pointed out, women often lose themselves in their relationships.[7] They may enable men to be irresponsible, destructive, or involved in substance abuse because they compromise themselves and their values to maintain the status quo. Some women so long to be loved and cared for by their partners that they mold themselves into whatever they believe is wanted of them. For women drawn into addictive, codependent relationships, healing is a process of making self-focused, responsible decisions. It is a process of taking control of your life, knowing that you can't control your loved one's actions or reactions.[8] For the woman with eating problems, it is a process of believing in herself enough to trust that her hungers are real and legitimate. Then she must feed the physical hunger and solve the relationship hunger separately.

Eating problems distort our relationships with one another and with God—yet relationships can be sources of healing for those struggles. Diane's problem with bulimia need not be published in the church bulletin prayer list, but Diane needs a committed prayer partner or a small group who can be used as a resource at any time. If she is in the middle of a crisis about food, talking to someone might help her through the crisis, enabling her to remember her desire to eat what she wants and needs. "Two or three gathered together" give strength against a problem. The prayer partner should not be an extra conscience or higher authority who tells her what to do but an equal with her, reminding her of God's love for her and of her own ability to act in a way that satisfies her own needs.

Ultimately, though, a woman must come face to face with her sense of self—who she is before God. God loves us just as we are, even when we don't feel very lovable or worthy. In our innermost selves we are made acceptable, not through our own acts or achievements, but through grace. We cannot prove our value by becoming the perfect shape or the perfect anything. When we get mired in repetitive cycles of self-condemnation, spiritual defeat, and food-focused thoughts, we need to remind ourselves that we can love ourselves because God loves us. And we can acknowledge ourselves as "saints in process," gifted with strength, power, and responsibility.

7.

Confronting Our
False Beliefs

Deidre believed that God wanted her to be thin. She fervently prayed every morning that God would take control of her eating. And every evening she cried and yelled at herself and at God for letting her be so gluttonous. This repetitive self-punishment alienated Deidre from God. It took months of constant challenge to her misguided belief—that God wanted her to be thin—to loosen her hatred of food, her shame of her body, and her mistrust of God.

Even if we have not been sexually victimized, even if we feel relatively in control of our lives, many of us are victimized in another way: we hate our bodies. We try diet after diet and nothing seems to work. We're stuck in repetitive cycles of thought that hold us back from making productive choices. We're victims of our own false beliefs.[1]

False Belief #1: Thin Is Beautiful

As we've already discussed, women today are under constant pressure to look perfect. The standards for the ideal female figure have become ever more stringent over the past several decades. A 1988 survey of the measurements of Miss America pageant winners and *Playboy* magazine centerfolds shows a sharp decline in weight/height proportion during the years from 1958 to 1978.[2] These women, who represent the American epitome of beauty and sexual appeal, were getting thinner and straighter as every year went on. The toothpaste-tube figure—as long and narrow as possible—was the ideal figure; the hourglass figure was out of fashion. But during that same time period, the average weight/height proportion for American women increased at about the same rate as the fashion models' proportions declined. In other words, real women were getting heavier as models were getting thinner. This discrepancy between real women and the ideal woman put exorbitant pressure on women to lose their curves in order to gain a sense of personal attractiveness, thus feeding the fervor for dieting.

Recently I had the opportunity to spend an afternoon sitting around a swimming pool at a hotel which was hosting a convention of salespeople from a major U.S. corporation. I was intrigued by the magazines the women were reading: *Vogue, Town and Country*, and *Cosmopolitan*, all full of predictably beautiful women. Yet only a handful of the women at the pool had body shapes that matched the models featured in the magazines, and most of them were teenagers. Real women don't look like fashion models. Fashion models don't look like the women we know.

Exercise:
Realistic
Body
Shapes

1. Check through any women's magazine and count the following:
☐ very thin women . . .
☐ thin women . . .
☐ medium women . . .
☐ heavy women . . .
☐ pregnant or breastfeeding women . . .
2. Situate yourself in a public place like a supermarket, airport, church, or PTA meeting. Count the women in the same categories:
☐ very thin women . . .
☐ thin women . . .
☐ medium women . . .
☐ heavy women . . .

□ pregnant or breastfeeding women . . .

3. What does the discrepancy in numbers say about real women in comparison to women in the media? Why do you think this discrepancy exists?

4. What did the process of categorization tell you about your own attitudes toward body size and shapes? Do your criteria for these evaluations change when you try to apply them to yourself?

Most Christian women believe, although we might never admit it aloud, that God wants women to be as thin as possible. And we believe that men want us to be that thin, too. Women are much tougher on their estimates of their own attractiveness than men are. When asked to judge which women men will find attractive, women point to pictures of women who are much thinner than the figures men actually choose.[3] When women think about their own ideal body size, they usually fantasize about a body that is very thin, very trim.

Most Christians have discarded the old legalisms that denounced makeup, jewelry, and slacks as immodest and worldly. Unfortunately we have replaced one simplistic mindset with another—an idolatry of the perfect body. One of the earliest theorists about body image, Hilde Bruch, pointed out the danger in this mix-up of values:

> It is impossible to assess the cost in serenity, relaxation, and efficiency of this abnormal, overslim, fashionable appearance. It produces serious psychological tensions to feel compelled to be thinner than one's natural make-up and style of living demand. There is a great deal of talk about the weakness and self-indulgence of overweight people who eat too much. Very little is said about the selfishness and self-indulgence involved in a life which makes one's appearance the center of all values and subordinates all

other considerations to it. I do not know how often people
are aware of the emotional sacrifice of staying slim.[4]

We must consciously, carefully, consistently give up the
notion, the subtle comment, the direct advice that says that to
be beautiful a woman must be thin. Any art history book
illustrates that the roundness and curves of the womanly form
have been admired throughout all time. Marilyn Monroe, one
of the sexiest women in movie history, was certainly no stick
figure. Elizabeth Taylor has lost and regained weight more
times than she's been married, yet she remains a star.

God wants us to be as authentically beautiful as possible,
but *that may not include being thin*. Beauty is not limited to body
shape, but develops from a sense of mystery, a sense of depth,
an overflow of grace that sparks a sense of fascination in
another person. It is a spiritual quality that shows through
when a woman is at ease with herself and dresses, grooms, and
cares for her physical self in her own distinctive way. Long-
term intimate relationships are maintained because a man likes
the way he feels about himself when he is with the woman he
loves; and women want to be loved as total persons, not just as
bodies. Relationships that depend on physical beauty won't
stand the test of time.

False Belief #2: Thin Is Sexy

If we perceive that thin women are more beautiful than
the average woman, it is easy to believe that they are more
sexually attractive, more likely to be worth loving. We can't
imagine a fat person having a fulfilling sex life or being a
satisfying sexual partner. But the truth is that sexual attraction
as experienced within the context of a loving, committed
relationship has little to do with thinness. Thinness does not
automatically lead to satisfying sexual relationships. Sidewalk
sexiness—earning a ten from men who admire you as you walk
down the sidewalk—may be enhanced by thinness, but this is
a distorted appreciation of sexuality.

Women become easily confused about the connections between thinness, sexuality, and relationships. Some women say that their passion goes into their eating and there's nothing left over for their intimate partners. As one woman explained it, "I'm more likely to get the 'hots' for a hot fudge sundae than for my husband." Other women point out that so much energy goes into worrying about their eating and what people are thinking about their bodies that they just don't care much about anything else.

> *Elizabeth explained to me that when her body was not trim and tight she felt unattractive, so it was impossible to see herself as sexually desirable to anyone. Even when her husband attempted to draw her into affectionate exchanges and lovemaking, she made up excuses to avoid his touching her body. She could not trust that he loved her, because she believed that her body made her unlovable. For Elizabeth this generalized body hatred grew so strong that she banned full-length mirrors from the house and would not let herself be seen in a bathing suit or underwear—even by her husband. Needless to say, when Elizabeth finally sought treatment her marriage was a shambles of broken trust, angry resentment, complete misunderstanding, and deep fears.*

Women who feel unattractive often become strangers to their bodies. They avoid looking at themselves. They won't join in games or sports because they fear their bodies will once again let them down. This disenchantment with one's body may gradually deepen with bitterness into self-hatred. All women with chaotic eating patterns must take on the process of making peace with their bodies, peace with their sexuality. This starts with becoming aware of one's body and then practicing affirming one's beauty.

Exercise:
Body
Awareness
and
Affirmation

1. What part of your body do you like the best? Why? How do you feel when you are using this part of your body? Has anyone ever told you this part of your body was beautiful?

2. What part of your body do you like the least? Why? How do you feel when you are using this part of your body? Has anyone ever told you this part was ugly?

3. Do these parts connect emotionally to any previous experience, any identification with family-shared characteristics, any experience of rejection, any change over time with age, any special meaning with children, or any sense of distinctiveness?

4. Recognize that your body is like no other. There is no room for comparison. God has made it special, unique in its beauty. Affirm your acceptance of all the parts of your body. Pull out the full length mirror in privacy and watch yourself move, bending, stretching, squatting, tightening and relaxing muscles all over your body. Practice touching, caring about, and being gentle with every part of yourself.

5. When you hear a comment rising that reflects self-disgust, body hatred, criticism, embarrassment at the way your body compares to other people's bodies, just breathe it out and let it pass. Focus on the affirmation: "This is my body and I cherish it. I am beautifully and wonderfully made. Thank you, God."

6. Ask your sexual partner to follow your directions and gently touch, stroke, and cherish all the parts of your body, slowly and carefully, without moving into sexual activity. Focus especially on the unlovable parts of your body.

7. If you do not already do so, involve your body in some sort of regular physical activity, some

movement experience, some exercise program that makes you feel good about your body.

When I assigned the "Body Awareness and Affirmation" exercise as counseling homework to Joanne, thirty-eight, she was resistant because she considered it silly. When I told her that I thought she was scared by it, she took it up as a challenge. Initially Joanne could only identify that she liked her little toe on her left foot, but didn't know why she even liked that piece of her body. After a few months of slow, grueling practice in body affirmation, working up to five minutes of stretching in front of the mirror a day, Joanne could identify several aspects of her body that she liked. This practice of celebrating her body was a key step in the healing of her eating disorder that was grounded in her self-hatred. As a side effect, her close relationships improved because as she felt more comfortable with her body, other people felt more comfortable in being near her.

In their struggle to be thin, women may unwittingly destroy intimate relationships. Women who participate in severe dieting, binge eating, or purging try to keep these secret because they suppose that people would be disgusted by their habits. So they become experts at hiding the evidence of their binges, timing their bathroom trips and toilet flushing with their vomiting, or eating in the middle of the night or other unexpected times. Husbands, parents, and friends usually know something is wrong but can't put a finger on the exact problem. Where there is not openness and honesty in a relationship, mistrust grows and love becomes distant and abstract. True intimacy cannot flourish in an atmosphere of secrets. So in the long run, thinness may make you look sexy at first glance, but it may actually sabotage your maintaining a mature sexual relationship.

False Belief #3: Thin Feels Better

Some women deny that they are oppressed by the need to be thin. They report that they just feel better, healthier, with more energy when they are thin. They feel good about themselves thin. But the snag is that they *only* feel good about themselves when they are thin.

> *Harriet had bouts of tremendous activity and a sense of well-being when she was in "good control" of her eating. When she was eating carefully she felt that she could move better, she looked better, people even liked her better. She was more productive at work and got along with her supervisors better when she was restrictively eating. At these times Harriet developed feelings of superiority over the other women whose eating was out of control. These positive self-reflections contrasted sharply with her typical self-image of an ugly, wrinkled, stretch-marked old woman who could never wear a pair of shorts on even the hottest day of the summer. While it is hard to begrudge Harriet her good feelings about herself, it is clear that her positive self-esteem was subtly but firmly rooted in her body size. When she started gaining weight her self-esteem plummeted.*

Our self-esteem should be rooted in God's valuing of us. We know that God does not judge us by our waist size. God cares about what we do, not how we look. When we are eating wrongly—that is, for reasons other than hunger—we may feel bad about ourselves. That self-evaluation is based on what we are *doing*, not how we are *looking*, and can motivate us to change what we do. The virtuous woman of Proverbs 31 is a doer, not a looker, not a dieter.

This woman does not sound like someone who sat around the house worrying about her weight. If you judge your success as a Christian on your weight, you are not meeting up to the standards of a virtuous woman. If feeling good about yourself depends on being thin—no matter how self-nurturantly you are eating—you've got a built-in self-esteem problem.

The "Self-Esteem History" exercise helps women identify the sources of their good feelings about themselves. As you do the exercise you should find that positive self-esteem rests on actions, on jobs that you did well, such as taking care of your newborn, successfully completing an important project at work, redecorating a room, or practicing ways to eat in response to hunger. If your "Self-Esteem History" directly parallels your weight history—if you're up when your weight is down and down when your weight is up—you are relying on a single, false criterion by which to value yourself.

Exercise:
Self-Esteem
History

1. Make a chart dividing your life into key periods, such as infancy, elementary school, high school, first job, early marriage, first child, last child, empty nest, menopause, postmenopause, retirement, widowhood, or any other divisions that make sense to your own timeline.
2. Reflect from an overall perspective how you felt about yourself during this time—content, energetic, anxious, excited, depressed.
3. What factors in your life cause you to feel this way? Were there any major ups or downs, and self-esteem boosters or crushers during this time?
4. Record average weight within each period. Note any dramatic shifts and the factors which cause major weight changes. Identify times of dieting, extreme exercising, purging, or other chaotic eating patterns.
5. Reflect on the following questions:
   ☐ Did self-esteem changes precede or follow weight change?
   ☐ Were there any times that you were heavy but happy? Why?
   ☐ Were there any times when you were thin and unhappy? Why?
   ☐ What factors in your life affect how you feel about yourself?

☐ Are you overly dependent on thinness to make you feel good about yourself?

☐ What else, for you, would be a better value on which to base your view of yourself?

One woman noted in doing this exercise that when her self-esteem dipped, her weight increased as a result. Her efforts to lower her weight seemed futile, but when she focused on her self-esteem, what built it up, what broke it down, she could take on a more effective and more healthy eating lifestyle. Another woman was surprised to see that there were times in her life when she was so active and feeling so fulfilled that her chronic anxiety about being overweight took a back seat. She could keep insecurity about her body in proper perspective, rather than becoming paralyzed and depressed about it.

It may take awhile to develop a healthy and balanced self-esteem, especially if a woman is unaccustomed to authentically claiming responsibility for her competencies. You need to inventory your strengths, your abilities, your accomplishments, and your positive personality characteristics. Try to evaluate yourself on your internal sense of yourself, not solely on what you think others think of you or to what degree you sense you are loved by other people. If you have difficulty identifying your strengths, ask a friend. Then validate his or her comments with your own internal sense that you do some things better than others. When you know what you are good at, you need to practice it. Do something satisfying, something effective, something challenging every day. Your self-respect grows as you take on productive, growth-oriented tasks that benefit others. As you see yourself in action, you come to appreciate your own distinctive way of doing things.

False Belief #4: Thin Is Spiritual

At the very core of our obsessions with food is the belief that God wants us to be thin—that God wants us to deny ourselves food. Disciplining our bodies, denying our appetites proves that we are spiritually mature. Eating reminds us that we are carnal, that we are earthly creatures, especially if we eat wrongly. Often people with eating problems have an underlying hatred of their own bodies. They would rather be all spirit.

These ideas reflect dualistic "body versus spirit" ideas that set up an unresolvable conflict between meeting bodily needs and meeting spiritual responsibilities. This false dualism is an old dilemma, a gnostic heresy dating back to the time of Christ when the New Testament community puzzled over the divine/human nature of Jesus. They wanted to deny his humanity just as we want to deny our fleshly weakness. But Jesus showed us a life that was fully human and fully divine— flesh and blood in union with spirit. Jesus accepted his physical self. We are told that he got tired, he felt pain, he washed feet, he accepted the woman's gift of perfume, and he wept. Surely Jesus enjoyed eating. Why else would he have told so many stories about food?

> Elise was a problem eater who got trapped in a cycle of fear and guilt, fear that she would lose control, guilt when she did lose control. Paradoxically, her "spiritual highs" occurred in those moments after a binge or a purge when she came face to face with her failure and cried out to God in an honest, deep way. At these moments of emotional outpouring, she experienced a keen awareness of God's love and concern for her and reported feeling good because she had "turned it all over to God." But she had turned over the wrong thing to God. She tried to dump her chaotic eating into God's lap without trusting God to clarify the misplaced feelings of fear and guilt that contributed to her problem.

Eating crises can motivate and energize life-changing patterns, or they can perpetuate a cycle of irresponsibility. Elise was keeping her focus limited to what she put in her mouth, rather than on the process of becoming a whole self, with body, mind, and emotions imbued with the Holy Spirit.

While some women overspiritualize eating and thinness,

some women deny that eating and spirituality are connected at all.

> Catherine, a pastor's kid, would binge during times of stress, when she had tough exams or conflict with her sister. After consuming a "mountain of calories" she would try to vomit. Sometimes when she felt that throwing up was "too gross" she would take half a bottle of milk of magnesia and crash on the couch. Catherine was experiencing an on-again, off-again personal relationship with God. Even in her moments of spiritual sensitivity, she kept her eating separate from her awareness of God. God cared about important things—like her anger at her parents, her lack of clarity about her future, and her love and loyalty to her friends—but not about her eating.

To Catherine, compulsive eating was a minor quirk that came and went during times of stress. She was unable to acknowledge that her difficulties with eating were compromising her connectedness to her spiritual life. While she thought she was keeping her eating in a separate, nonspiritual sphere, her chaotic eating was subtly but steadily eroding her trust in God's ability to meet her needs in time of stress.

Dieting does not make one more spiritual or obedient. Food is not bad; it is given to us as a good gift from God. Eating can bring us satisfaction, relief from hunger, and connectedness to our own bodies, our own sexuality. Thinness is not next to godliness. We need not punish our bodies into submission. While misguided beliefs about thinness lead us to victimize ourselves, self-nurturant eating keeps our bodies and spirits alive.

8.

God Cares How You Eat

As the pastor told the story of the feeding of the five thousand, Emma daydreamed about a diet of "loaves"—preferably that good bakery Italian bread—where she would miraculously eat all the food she wanted but never gain weight. As the pastor asked the congregation to stand for the closing hymn, she concluded that the Bible had nothing to say about her problem with food except when it chastised her for fleshly lusts, weakness, and disobedience. It certainly did not offer a feasible diet plan!

A common assumption among Christians could be summed up: "I can't remember ever hearing a sermon about eating, so there must not be anything important in the Bible about eating." Eating seems too mundane, even embarrassing an issue to merit attention from the preachers in our pulpits. Yet eating food is perhaps the most commonly used biblical metaphor to explain God's care for us and our responsibility to God.

Eating is personal, intimate, and immediate. According to Scripture, we should eat to satisy hunger and nourish our bodies, to build trust within our community, and to symbolize our spiritual commitment. Eating is a reflection of our lives as Christians, and we are responsible for nutritionally adequate and spiritually sensitive eating. In eating, we demonstrate our awareness of God's provision for our needs and our respect for our bodies as temples of the Holy Spirit. God cares how we eat.

God's Gift of Hunger

God created hunger to tell us when to eat. Satisfying our hunger with food strengthens our body. Eating is meant to be a physically, emotionally, socially, and spiritually satisfying experience. Jesus said as much himself in Matthew 12:1-4, 6-7:

> *At that time Jesus went through the grainfields on the Sabbath. His disciples were hungry and began to pick some heads of grain and eat them. When the Pharisees saw this, they said to him, "Look! Your disciples are doing what is unlawful on the Sabbath." He answered, "Haven't you read what David did when he and his companions were hungry? He entered the house of God, and he and his companions ate the consecrated bread—which was not lawful for them to do, but only for the priests. . . . I tell you that one greater than the temple is here. If you had known what these words mean, 'I desire mercy, not sacrifice,' you would not have condemned the innocent."*

While this is a complicated story to interpret within its historical and spiritual context, it points out that responding to hunger is a good reason for eating. The disciples' actions were justified because they were hungry and needed food. The ecclesiastical rules were eclipsed by their need for food. All the external rules we devise about eating—when to eat, what not to eat, how many calories to consume, which foods to avoid— do not matter if we are eating because we are hungry. Eating should be a physically satisfying, invigorating experience. If it isn't, something is wrong with the way we are eating.

Where Two or Three Are Eating . . .

The Bible shows us that eating together symbolizes community. Sharing food connects people to each other and develops honesty and trust at a deep level. Jesus used social eating both to reach out to sinners and to build up his community of faith. Remember how scandalized the Pharisees felt when they saw Jesus eating with tax collectors and sinners? This episode of eating was sensational enough to be repeated in three Gospels (Matt. 9:11; Mark 2:16; Luke 15:2) and in two of them is followed up by complaints from the Pharisees that the disciples didn't fast often or severely enough. Jesus understood that eating together breaks down barriers and establishes trust between people. Sometimes the most effective communication occurs at the kitchen table over that second cup of coffee and the fresh muffin.

One of the most tender scenes of Jesus as Foodgiver occurs after his resurrection as he stands on the beach when the disciples have fished all night but have caught nothing. He instructs them how to catch the fish and when they reach the shore, they find fish and bread already cooking. As he feeds them, he confirms their allegiance to him ("Do you love me?") and passes on his commission to them ("Feed my sheep"). His metaphor of nourishment binds together this motley crew of disciples in a way that speeches, chiding, and testing could not.

In our own communities of faith, food still maintains its power to build up connections across barriers of all sorts. Coffee hour after church, potluck dinners, the Sunday school picnic, prayer breakfasts, and love feasts—all these eating events make it easier to share together on a deeper level. It particularly spotlights the gifts of those women who can bake a great cherry pie but would never take on a more outspoken teaching or preaching ministry in the church. One multicultural church ministry is thriving, partly because the people delight in sharing their ethnic foods—collard greens, tabbouleh, Creole rice, and quesadillas. In so doing, they are also sharing their traditions, their histories, and their identities with one another. Those with a more conservative palate have made the effort to accept graciously these food offerings. In this way, eating creates a bond of trust. It also demonstrates concern for others in making sure that all present, even those who bring only their hunger, are well fed within the community of faith.

The New Testament also gives us an example of destructive eating. Particularly in the Corinthian community, eating meat previously offered to idols became a controversial decision, based not on the health of the meat itself, but on other people's attitudes toward the eating. Paul writes: "Food will not bring us close to God. We are no worse off if we do not eat, and no better off if we do. . . . Therefore, if food is a cause of their falling, I will never eat meat, so that I may not cause one of them to fall" (1 Cor. 8:8, 13 NRSV).

Conflicts about eating and drinking still occur in the Christian church of the twentieth century. While the Bible does not offer us easy answers, it does indicate that, if the issue of consuming or abstaining becomes a stumbling block to the faith of a community member, it should be addressed directly with the goal of a negotiated compromise or abstinence in the presence of the offended person.

There are times the church can overdo eating. I recall a church-sponsored teenage banquet serving fancy, expensive foods—some of which ended up on the floor after a food fight finale. Extravagance and waste of food runs counter to our responsibility to feed the world. American wastefulness contributes to world hunger and poverty. The typical American's craving for coffee, chocolate, and sugar products supports large-scale Latin American plantations where the profits go to the landowner, rather than smaller subsistence farms growing staples to feed the members of that impoverished community. As Christians, we must eat with an awareness of the hunger needs evident in the rest of the world. One of our favorite resources for cooking and eating responsibly is the *More-with-Less Cookbook*. Published by the Mennonites, it emphasizes economical, creative recipes with an international flair.[1]

Free to Feast

Ritual often depends on food. Feasting and fasting were major ways in the Old Testament to celebrate a significant event in Jewish history, to provide a welcome, to give thanksgiving, or to demonstrate repentance. Recall the food rituals and extensive dietary laws of the Hebrews in the Old Testament. Their laws governing food established their identity as members of a community and separated them from their pagan neighbors. In the New Testament, Jesus demonstrated in the Last Supper the most profound use of food as a symbol of communion with him. Holy Communion replicates in the bread and wine our decision to incorporate Jesus into the very innermost parts of ourselves and ourselves into the body of Christ.

We also use food for rituals in our culture. We celebrate birthdays with cake and ice cream. When two people marry, they often feed cake to each other. Families develop favorite feast foods. The church calendar, with its transitions from Advent to Christmas to Lent to Easter to Pentecost, involves food traditions that go far back in time, like hot cross buns, potato pancakes, fruitcakes, pretzels, and mincemeat—all bringing to mind some part of the Judeo-Christian story. Evelyn Birge Vitz, in *A Continual Feast*, shares recipes that honor food within Christian tradition.[2] For some women, establishing religiously-based feasts may transform food from an enemy to be fought and feared to an enjoyable experience, reconnecting them to themselves and God.

God Provides!

God's clearest directions about eating came to the people of Israel while they were sojourning in the wilderness on their way from Egypt to the Promised Land. The story in Exodus 16 starts with the whole congregation grumbling to Moses about their discomfort and hunger. They had a lot to learn about God's provision for them.

> *"If only we had died by the LORD's hand in Egypt! There we sat around pots of meat and ate all the food we wanted, but you have brought us out into this desert to starve this entire assembly to death." (Exod. 16:3)*

That whining motif echoes throughout the whole story of the Exodus. Because we know what happened next, it is difficult to take their complaints seriously. Those of us with well-stocked pantries do not really know the panic born of hunger. One cannot think about God when one is hungry. We must respond to people's physical pains and hunger if we expect them to hear the Gospel. Even when we are not starving, excessive concern about food and eating obscures our spiritual vision. You cannot see God when your mind is filled with calorie counting or visions of hot fudge sundaes.

Our God meets our needs. God responded to the most basic human needs of the Israelites by "raining down bread from heaven" with the morning dew. The people gathered up what they needed of the small, seed-like manna, and when the sun came, the manna melted away. In this way, they received a daily reminder of God's goodness to them. In our own life, we forget that food is a gift from God. We may thank God at every meal for our food, but our thanks has become routine. When we hate our eating, we may find it impossible to sincerely thank God for the gift of food. So we withhold our thanks, or we mouth the words without the awareness of God's love for us.

The people of Israel were supplied with more food than they could use. They could pick up whatever they needed each day. At first many probably worried about God's provision, so they tried to gather extra manna, just in case God did not come through on those heavenly promises. But manna that was hoarded just rotted away. People collecting manna learned quickly to gauge accurately how much food would satisfy their family's hunger. Hoarding food was unnecessary and did not make them more secure, just as filling our freezers doesn't make us safe. Saving up food was honored only as preparation for the Sabbath, when time was devoted to glorifying God and not to cooking activities. Far too often we spend too much time in the kitchen preparing a meal intended to draw family members together rather than focusing our family time on providing a resting space in which to let God nurture us.

What? Manna Again?

The manna was satisfying to the people's hunger. It is described as the "bread of angels" and "grain of heaven" (Ps. 78:24–25). It was a versatile grain that could be beaten with a mortar and pestle and made into a paste that became the basis of breads and cakes (Num. 11:8). The people of Israel relied on this highly nutritious manna for survival.

For us, it is hard to imagine grocery shopping for one thing: manna. We cannot believe that it could be satisfying for long. We would not consider making the same recipe twice in a week. And we complain about leftovers which too often sit in the refrigerator until thrown away.

The great variety of foods available to us often lures us into eating in an unhealthy way. There is too much to choose from, so we taste a bit of everything. A missionary friend home on furlough from Eastern Europe was overwhelmed by the forty-seven kinds of cereal she found in one store, a dramatic contrast to the block-long bread lines in Poland. Overflowing supermarkets cause overflowing shopping bags which cause overflowing plates which cause overflowing stomachs.

Most of us humans have an appreciation of international cuisine and fancy restaurants, and it is normal to want to try different foods. But sometimes in our quest for novel tastes and textures, we neglect basic, elemental, generally healthier foods. It seems easy to pop a prepared "lite" entree with a mouth-watering picture on the package into the microwave, but we neglect to examine the label to find those lowest in sodium, sugar, preservatives, or additives. We sacrifice nutrition to convenience. Good eating need not be boring, nor should it be gourmet fare every day. It should be nutritious, pleasurable, and economical. Although nutritious eating may take some effort at first, it quickly becomes easier and more satisfying. Food which is closest to the way God made it is probably the all-round best food for us to eat.

Forty years is a long time in which to subsist on a limited diet, so it is not surprising that some of the Israelites started complaining about the menu after awhile. "We remember the fish we ate in Egypt at no cost—also the cucumbers, melons, leeks, onions and garlic. But now we have lost our appetite; we never see anything but this manna!" (Num. 11:5–6). God went on to provide meat to the people but warned them that it would be consumed for thirty days until it "comes out of your nostrils and you loathe it" (Num. 11:20). It is recorded that many of those who lusted for meat, whose physical appetite caused them to sin, died from infectious disease caused by that meat.

Scriptures such as this lead some people toward becoming vegetarian. Others identify scruples about killing animals, convictions about preserving world resources, or personal health reasons as the basis for abstaining from meats. Daniel and his friends Shadrach, Meshach, and Abednego, chosen by Nebuchadnezzar for court life, refused to eat the portion of the king's meat or his wine. They submitted themselves to a comparison testing, eating vegetables and grain, and "At the end of the ten days they looked healthier and better nourished than any of the young men who ate the royal food" (Dan. 1:15). While not all Christians need become vegetarians, decreasing our consumption of meat (especially red meat) and returning to simple, wholesome food choices from the four basic food groups is generally healthier and more satisfying.

Food that is eaten without God's endorsement and blessing does not nourish us. It makes us sick. People who experience hypersensitive responses to food, for example, being allergic to strawberries or chocolate, should respect the messages they receive from their bodies about those food choices. Our bodies know best what we need, if we can develop the sensitivity to listen to them. When we habitually experience food as sickening, we may be eating in a way that is unbiblical. Food is meant to be satisfying and healthful for us.

Feed Us First with Spiritual Food

We are told that all the Israelites "ate the bread of angels" (Ps. 78:25). Moses, the leader of the tribe, ate the same meal as his followers. Eating manna was a unifying, distinction-erasing experience. The manna signifies the grace freely available to all in the true Bread of Life, Jesus Christ—of which we can all choose to eat. Wholesome eating is a symbol of redemption, spiritual unity, and restoration to wholeness in every part of our being. Spiritual nourishment must be our first priority.

When eating, when being in good shape becomes too important to us, we lose sight of the personal vision to which God calls us. The Israelites wandered in the wilderness for forty years because their concerns about eating, drinking, and daily comforts took priority over the vision of the Promised Land. When you find yourself wandering through the day from snacks to meals to calorie counting to fancy self-lectures about food, you know you need to regain your vision of the Promised Land.

Exercise:
Manna for
Today

How does your eating measure up against the Israelites' experience with manna? Do you

☐ feel nourished by the food you eat?
☐ spend too much time worrying about eating?
☐ find it easy to thank God for the food you eat?
☐ hoard food or eat in secret?
☐ complain about the food you eat?
☐ relish memories of old eating experiences?
☐ regularly examine labels to evaluate quality?
☐ weekly try a nutritious new recipe or new dish?
☐ emphasize natural, unprocessed food in your eating?
☐ find eating boring?
☐ stay sensitive to your special responses to food?

□ change your eating pattern to honor the Sabbath?

□ let food obscure your personal vision for the future?

"Lord, Where Are You?"

Prolonged turmoil about eating alienates us from God. We lose our awareness of God's abiding presence in our lives. Increasingly, women with eating problems become mired in the here and now of their bodies. This entry from Cindy's prayer journal captures the spiritual numbness of that experience:

Lord, where are you? I am in a fog and only can cognitively know by Scripture that you will not forsake me. I had made a good resolve on Friday to start taking care of myself. I now do not have the desire to follow through. My emotions have died and I imagine my body may follow. I don't feel your love.

Women like Cindy may sincerely believe in the power of God. But they cannot appropriate that power for themselves to help them achieve peace in this area of their lives. Their faith is secure only as long as it stays in their heads and doesn't come near their bodies, and their faith suffers when they despair over their eating. In order to change their eating patterns, they first need to feel God's love and hope.

When I first started meeting with Sandra, she repeated frequently that she hated herself because she was so fat. When I pointed out that if she hates herself, it must be hard to believe that God loves her, she broke into tears. Sandra started to practice saying daily, as a point of faith, that God loved her just as she was. We combined this with looking in the mirror at her body—especially those problematic spots like her thighs, upper arms, and stomach—and affirming that God loved this part of her, too. Gradually that head knowledge turned to heart knowledge. Sandra experienced the warmth of self-acceptance, and consequently she was able to eat more consciously and more responsibly.

The Right Kind of Praying

Chaotic eating produces spiritual chaos. Christian women with eating problems bounce between spiritual success and spiritual despair. This chaos shows most clearly in their prayer life. When they are in control of food or are consistently dieting, they can pray easily. When they feel fat or out of control or are obsessed with the desire to binge, their prayer may be limited to frantic "desperation" prayers. If they are wanting to binge, they pray "Lord, help me stay in control" and if they have just binged it is "Lord, forgive me and help me get in control."

Prayer about chaotic eating can be effective only when it is in tune with God's plan for our eating. When we pray only in reaction to our behaviors and mistakes, we become frustrated. Working out in advance a personal and preventive prayer about eating can be helpful for women with troubled prayer lives and troubled eating.

> *Gracious God, I know that you love me right now. I know that you want me to feel satisfied in all aspects of my life. Thank you for feeding me with your spiritual food and physical food. Guide my food choices in these next few hours, that I will eat, conscious of your presence and my own hunger. Help me to love my body as it is. If I make mistakes, it's okay because I am trying hard from the inside out—and you love me all the time, any way I am.*

If People Only Knew the Real Me . . .

Even though many Christians with eating problems experience spiritual poverty or internal chaos, they may outwardly look like strong Christians. They may be the leaders in the congregation, the organizers for church suppers, the church secretaries, the energetic, committed young people. Or they may prefer to work quietly behind the scenes, thus avoiding intense one-on-one interaction with others while remaining heavily involved in the work of God. Only when you stop to talk with them—not just work along beside them—can you recognize their emotional needs.

Charlotte was such a person—respected by her acquaintances for her Christian walk but a chaotic eater who was lonely and self-critical. She continually judged herself, how she looked, what others might say about her. Our counseling sessions were full of reports that despite her external successes, she feared people would discover her internal unworthiness and discredit her. Her fears spurred her to doing more and more good works, which only made her feel more empty. Charlotte finally recognized that she was a puppet of her conflicts and took seriously her need to share her vulnerability with her Christian friends. When she shared the story of her chaotic eating, her friends and family did not reject her. As they accepted her, it became easier for her to accept herself. As she became more honest and open, her life as a Christian became more integrated and real. She was able to use these friends as buffers during times of eating crises and encouragers when her motivation to struggle with her chaotic eating was low.

God Can Begin a New Work in My Life!

As Christians we know that God's grace is sufficient to meet our needs and nurture us toward spiritual maturity. But it is often difficult to put that faith into practice. For many women with eating problems, building faith in action requires them to return to their most basic beliefs about God and themselves. The counselor or family member who wants to help her must often reaffirm basic spiritual principles and primary beliefs, even for the woman who seems so mature and who has taken on a major leadership position in the church. She can then remember and reexperience the love of God and the realities of God at work in every part of her life.

The eating-troubled woman needs to know that God wants good things for her. She needs to begin to look and listen inside herself rather than to look to other people; she needs to hear God speaking to her; and she must make a decision about whether or not she will choose to grow in God. In doing so, she is deciding to be responsive to God's individual call in her life.

God wants us to be productive, responsible disciples who are becoming more and more Christlike in all that we do. Our chaotic eating can too easily unsettle our faith and consume all our attention and energy. Read again, from this perspective, Matthew 6:25, 31–33 (modified):

> *"Therefore I tell you, do not worry about your life, what you will eat or drink; or about your body, what you will wear. Is not life more important than food, and the body more important than clothes? . . . So do not worry, saying, 'What shall we eat?' or 'What shall we drink?' or 'What shall we wear?' For the pagans run after all these things, and God knows that you need them. But seek first the kingdom and righteousness of God, and all these things will be given to you as well."*

Exercise: What Does the Bible Say?

This exercise is designed to help you identify the biblical sources and teachings you have heard about eating, and to reexamine the importance and meaning of food in specific Bible passages.

1. Make a list from memory of Bible stories, situations, and references that mention food, hunger, or eating.

2. Choose three and recall from memory what that Scripture passage said about food and eating.

3. Locate and read carefully the Scripture passages. If you can't remember where to find the story, use a concordance, which will help you trace a key word throughout the Bible. While you have the concordance out, note the extensive list of biblical references for the word "eat."

4. What was the food in the passage? Was there enough of it, or too little? What was the historical and situational context of the section? Was this an individual or a group experience with eating? How does this affect the story? What is your impression of the people who eat or hunger in this story? How important was food in the passage? What does the passage say about the process of eating? Did the story represent a conflict about eating? What was it? What was the emotional meaning of the food in the story? Where was the hunger in the story? How was it met? Or was the hunger never satisfied?

5. What was the spiritual meaning of food in the story? What did it symbolize? What practical lessons about eating can be drawn from this Scripture? What spiritual lessons?

6. Did your memory of the story's message about food match what was said in the passage? If not, why do you suppose you recalled it in a distorted way? How could you interpret this Scripture in a way to support healthy eating patterns? How does this Scripture provide resources for constructive spiritual growth?

9. Eating Our Way Through Life

My mother is on a diet to lose forty pounds; my sister is pregnant and struggling not to gain too much weight; the doctor says my dad has to lose weight—but of course he eats as much greasy food as ever; our freezer is stuffed with Weight-Watchers products, frozen french fries, and gourmet ice cream—and you want me to eat more sensibly?
—Jennifer, age twenty-one

From infancy on, through our parents' example, through direct teaching, through all kinds of messages and experiences, we absorb certain lessons about eating. Is food readily available? Can we snack any time or are certain foods rationed? Is food the panacea, whatever the pain? Is someone always dieting? Is food equated with love? Do we receive subtle messages about our own self-worth? As Carla says, "My mom begs me to come see her and I do believe, in her own way, she loves me, but the message I always heard growing up was, 'You're too fat.' I don't always want to see her."

Our relationship with food changes over time. When we're teenagers, we tend to obsess over the state of our bodies. Such obsessions may lead us to deny our bodies' needs and go hungry most of the time. Or we eat too much, or eat the wrong things. Or, more positively and with the help of our families, we may be enabled to listen to our changing bodies and nurture them well, enjoying our expanding skills and circles of relationships. In adulthood, eating may be our means of taking care of ourselves; feeding others may mean expressing love, or may be one more experience of being taken for granted. Shared experiences of feeding others may be particularly meaningful or, for others of us, traumatic. When I participated in a recent wedding, I appreciated the delight one woman took in making white chocolate heart candies for the reception, her gift to the bride and groom—and, being a chocolate lover, I too enjoyed her gift.

As our attitudes change with age, our bodies are also changing. The biological changes in puberty, pregnancy, childbirth, and menopause affect our eating and our attitudes toward food and ourselves. Awareness of the psychological and biological changes that take place for men and women throughout the lifespan makes it easier to understand the roots of eating problems—and how to solve those problems.

Infancy: The Right Kind of Nurture

Feeding an infant is the most elemental act of nurture one can provide. One literally sustains the child's life by giving food. Beyond basic sustenance, however, parents need to learn to recognize, correctly interpret, and meet their child's needs. Parents who are overly intrusive or who feed their child in response to every need, whether it is for food or not, hinder their child's growth, making it more difficult for the child to know her own needs or to appropriately meet them later on. Some parents try to force their child to eat more than she wants; others try to restrict eating. Children may therefore learn to eat long past when they feel hungry, or they may learn to stop eating before they are full. The quality of the parent-infant relationship teaches children the meaning of food and the importance of their needs.

Responsive parents want to feed their children when they are hungry, and feed them well. They may choose to limit the sweets their infant eats, and it is appropriate to restrict colas, candies, and other snack foods with limited nutritional value. Recently, however, our obsession with dieting has extended to infants, with serious negative effects. Standing in line with the mother of a seven-month-old, I was surprised to hear her apologize for her baby's large size. Indeed, most babies become chunky just before they begin crawling or walking. Yet some well-meaning parents, concerned about obesity, have begun limiting their infant's intake of necessary nutrients. These parents provide their infants skim milk. They encourage complex carbohydrates and try to limit fats, salt, and sugar. This model of eating, although recommended for adults, is harmful to children under two years of age. Pediatricians have documented failures in normal growth as a result. Infants should not be given low-fat foods, as fat-containing foods often contain valuable nutrients for children, such as iron and calcium. They need some sugar and can benefit from healthy snacks.

Some infants may have trouble at first with feeding or digesting their food. Premature infants have immature digestive systems, and full-term infants also differ in their digestive maturity. Infants may need to feed for a long time (because of a weak suck, perhaps) or may need to drink more milk than the mother provides or may have colic, making them difficult to quiet. These early frustrations in feeding are normal for many children and, if the issues have been discussed with their pediatrician, parents should realize that they need not contribute to long-term eating problems.

Children begin to explore independence, with food and in other ways, in infancy. As the mother of a two-year-old recently said, "I miss the calm days of breast-feeding. Now I'm running back and forth from the dining room to the kitchen, getting her food, cleaning up her spills, deciding when to encourage her to eat and when to ignore it." Just as children experiment with dropping toys, or putting things in their mouths, or walking, they experiment with spitting, and turning away from food, and playing in their food. During infancy, children learn to feed themselves and begin to substitute solid for liquid foods. At the same time, parent and child are getting to know one another and trying out different feeding techniques. By the end of infancy, things get more complicated, as we shall see.

Toddlerhood: The Mealtime Battleground

During the toddler years, as the child learns to say no, she says no to food and mealtimes, as well as to other activities. Parents often label this period as the "terrible twos." They may begin to describe mealtimes as a struggle. Deborah is home full-time with her toddler and infant sons. Mealtimes are particularly difficult for her, as the older child often refuses to eat. Deborah has developed a pattern of pushing food, preparing his ever-changing "favorites," encouraging him repeatedly to eat, following him from room to room enticing him with morsels of food, and punishing him for wasting and refusing food.

Infants, particularly young infants, should be fed on demand, but toddlers and preschool children seem to need some regularity in their schedule, and have more trouble when, for example, the evening meal is sometimes served at 5:00 and at other times at 8:30. Children should not generally be allowed to watch television or play games as they eat, because they need to learn to pay attention to their body signals. Parents should make the effort to eat with children, helping them to experience food as a rewarding, shared family activity.

Feeding toddlers depends on satisfying *their* hunger, not the parent's hunger, and encouraging them to make their own choices (but not allowing too many choices). Be sure they are not dulling their appetite by drinking continuously from an ever-present bottle. Recognize that they eat erratically, consuming large amounts of food at some times and little at others. Many parents formerly taught children to "clean your plate," but children can learn to gauge and satisfy internal hungers if they have some degree of control over food intake. If parents can be somewhat firm yet flexible, with a generous dose of humor, they may be able to avoid major struggles with eating and help children develop awareness of their internal cues for hunger.

Preschool Age: The Beginnings of Independence

During the preschool years, children become progressively able to find food and feed themselves. They know how to open the refrigerator, toast the bread, find the peanut butter. They delight in their increased competence and independence, and they are developing a mind of their own. Children may start playing with food, dawdling, and refusing food even more than before. Parents may find setting limits difficult, and can make it easier for themselves by changing the setting to limit distractions and alternative choices for foods. Desserts should be contingent on at least trying a few bites of every food served. Have some freely available foods, carrots, olives, peanut butter, or whatever the child likes, to teach children to modulate their own eating.

During these years, children also begin to learn what it means to be male and female. Girls may be encouraged to help feed the family, whereas boys participate little in the process. Differing expectations of boys and girls set the stage for their adult life and may begin to teach girls that food has a dominant place in women's lives. As a result, girls may learn to express their struggles and satisfy their needs through food more often than boys. Both boys and girls can be encouraged to help in the kitchen, and parents can use this time and mealtimes to talk about their children's lives and encourage their sharing.

Preschoolers are already absorbing our culture's messages about thin and fat in ways that can be detrimental in their own development. My own daughter, at age four, reported that she didn't want peanut butter in her sandwich because her daycare teacher wouldn't eat peanut butter because it was fattening. The message that being fat was horrible came across loud and clear.

I was told a humorous, true story about two preschoolers who heard their mother complaining about her fat and decided to help her out. Early in the morning, they crept into her bedroom with the longest pin they could find and jammed it into her thigh. They envisioned that, when she stopped whooshing around the room like a leaking balloon, she would be thin. What a disillusioning incident!—but one that marks the sensitivity and awareness that youngsters have for adult attitudes about their bodies.

School Age: The Youngest Dieters

During the school years, children begin to explore various foods, especially as a result of peer relationships, and perhaps to learn to cook. Familial attitudes toward food become deeply ingrained. One seven-year-old girl, Susan, ate only peanut butter and Triscuits. She ate alone while her mother, a recovering bulimic, and father ate together after she went to bed. The little girl had learned that eating was shameful and a lonely experience. When she started school, her friends invited her to their houses and she began to see other ways of eating— and to struggle with her own social eating. In therapy, she began to enjoy shared food experiences such as baking cookies, making orange juice, and exploring new flavors of frozen yogurt. Although she'll probably never be a liberal eater, she has broadened her eating and her understanding of food.

The school-age years are the prime years for skill development. Children enjoy making a product and doing a good job. They delight in activity and should be encouraged, within reason, to participate in their own feeding and food preparation. School lunches may become the focus of struggle. Parents should encourage children to eat in the cafeteria, when possible, as cafeteria lunches must meet federal standards for nutrition, and bag lunches often are not as nutritious or as well balanced, providing higher fat content.

Concerns about eating and weight are increasingly frequent among school-aged children, and overwhelmingly so among girls. Eating disorders may appear in children as young as eight or nine years of age. In a recent survey in San

Francisco, thirty-one percent of nine-year-olds expressed concern that they were or might become fat. Almost half the nine-year-olds and eighty percent of the ten- and eleven-year-olds have dieted.

My youngest client who requested a diet was eight. Her father was a chef at a local, exclusive restaurant, and her mother was significantly depressed and overwhelmed with working a full-time job and caring for their child so many evenings alone. This child's life had become so centered around food that she had dropped her after-school activities and lost contact with many of her friends so she could come home and eat. Although the child's weight was not out of range for her age, she had already learned the importance society places on weight.

Children whose parents divorce may express their concerns through their eating. Children at these ages generally realize that they are not to blame for the divorce. Yet they may feel abandoned and may deny themselves food or overeat as an expression of their need for nurturance. Parents can help their children through these crises by providing balanced meals on a relatively regular schedule, by encouraging their children to talk about their concerns, and by providing healthy food for snack foods.

Obesity in children is an increasing problem. Dr. William Dietz of the New England Medical Center documented a five percent increase in obesity among children ages six to eleven in the last twenty years and a thirty-nine percent rise in obesity among adolescents twelve to seventeen.[1] In other words, the average weight gain is greater than it was in previous years. More children are obese, and the fat are becoming more fat. The earlier one develops obesity, the more one is likely to weigh as an adult. Obese children become more obese than adults who first gain weight in adulthood.

There are a variety of reasons for the rise in obese children. We live in an eating-disordered society, in which families too often eat chaotically. Most of us eat foods higher in fats than did earlier generations. Because of conflicting schedules, families may not eat together regularly or may frequent fast-food chains. Children may be left to fend for themselves, missing out on good nutrition. Television and Nintendo provide too ready a baby-sitter, and children sit passively watching endless ads for high carbohydrate, high-sugar foods. Poor eating habits and obesity are no surprise in such a culture.

Obesity should not be ignored, but dieting alone is not the answer. Children need to develop early on a lifestyle of health that includes a range of activities and experiences, with appropriate opportunities for eating and exercise.

Parents who want to encourage positive eating habits in children should:

1. Pay attention to how you use food. For example, do you use it to soothe physical hurts? Feed by the child's hunger, not yours.
2. Allow children some choice in variety, amount, and type of food but don't become a "short order cook" providing limitless choices and cooking on demand.[2]
3. Don't use food as a reward or punishment.
4. Encourage vigorous physical activity.
5. Don't let mealtimes become a struggle.
6. Limit television. Encourage instead your child's development of a range of interests, friends, and activities.
7. Keep your sense of humor, and go for help when you need it.

Adolescence: Developing Confidence and Self-esteem

In adolescence, girls feel strong peer pressure to be thin, and most girls go on a diet. Yet dieting runs counter to the normal biological changes in hormonal and sexual development that occur during this time. While girls are biologically preprogrammed to be putting on weight, current fashion encourages them to lose weight.

Teenage girls should be encouraged to be realistic about

their weight and to recognize the unrealistic demands of their peers. Parents can also encourage their daughters to view their lives wholistically. Teenage girls are prone to dichotomous thinking ("If I were thinner, he'd go out with me.") There are many characteristics of one's life that affect relationships, and parents can encourage their daughters to recognize their strengths and to focus on characteristics other than weight as bases for relationships.

Parents should *not* encourage their early teenage daughters to go on a diet. Almost all children who are approaching adolescence become pudgy. Their bodies are preparing for a growth spurt, and parents should not overreact to this. Negative comments will teach girls that their body is unacceptable. Further, dieting is dangerous. A teenager who diets severely may begin the sad cycle of dieting and gaining weight, sucked into a lifestyle that is ultimately self-defeating. Parents are wiser to encourage their daughters to begin to exercise moderately, if they do not already do so, and to develop better relationships and activities to occupy their interests and time.

Adolescence is the primary era of identity development, and the major issues of adolescence—separation, independence, intimacy, and sexuality—are central to this process. Eating becomes a vehicle for the expression of these issues, and their inappropriate resolution can lead to the development of eating disorders. For example, overly conforming children in early adolescence feel ambivalent about the necessary struggles for autonomy and avoid these as long as possible. They may express them only in refusing to eat what their parents have provided for them, a pattern that is characteristic of anorexics. Teenagers who resent parental authority may refuse parental nurturance by insisting on fast foods, rather than eating the food provided them at home. Bulimics may binge in reaction to conflicts with parents, eating excessively when they feel cared for at home, not eating when they feel angry with their parents or peers, or vice versa. Sexuality, too, is closely identified with eating. Teenagers may diet to attract boys or diet excessively to prevent the development of adolescent curves and avoid the attention of teenage boys.

Teenagers often develop an identity that centers on their weight or their eating habits. They may see themselves as "fat and unattractive" or "thin and sexy." They may feel "out of control" around food, developing a sense of themselves that is similarly powerless and self-abusive, or "in control" and self-confident. Appropriate identity development should include a positive sense of oneself as being attractive and competent, with an awareness of the importance of eating but without feeling controlled by it, with weight as part of one's identity but not its dominating feature.

Young Adulthood and the College Years: On Their Own

With young adulthood, women and men consolidate their sense of self. If their identity includes eating in unhealthy ways, these attitudes prove difficult to change. Maritza, a college sophomore, wails, "All my friends say I eat badly—I eat one meal a day, usually late at night, and it's usually a pizza or a sub. I've *always* eaten this way and never noticed other people didn't. It's the only way I know how to eat."

The search for intimacy in young adulthood may make food of continuing or increasing importance. In our society, women who have difficulty with relationships or who delay marrying fear being deemed unattractive or overweight. One competent, single woman in her early thirties said that, as long as she knew people viewed her as thin and attractive, her single state (despite her desire to marry) was less vulnerable to criticism.

The college years bring new challenges in eating: eating solo or with friends, in the college cafeteria or one's own apartment. Pressures to diet may be especially strong. College women readily teach one another the latest diet and encourage weight loss. In a recent study of college-aged men and women at a Christian college, two-thirds of the women surveyed and one-fifth of the men were concerned with their weight. Concerns with weight are "significant," even among those who report that their weight is "just right" for their height. Women appear somewhat aware that their expectations for their weight are unrealistic. Almost half the women who believe their weight is "just right" want to lose as much as five to fifteen pounds.[3]

Marriage: New Relationships, New Problems

Marriage opens up an exciting new chapter for women and men but also raises new issues related to eating. Some of the most common questions about a new couple's life together are: "Can she cook?" "Is she feeding you well?" Indeed, our cultural stereotype is that men gain weight when they marry, implying that they have been poorly cared for before marriage and are unable to care for themselves. The reality is the opposite: Women (on the average) gain more weight than men when they marry, perhaps because they feel they have been "chosen" and no longer need to compete for men.

Many married women struggle with finding control and meaning in a society that devalues women, particularly if they do not work outside the home. Some women feel that in marriage they have few choices about where to live or what to do. Having children also diminishes many women's sense of self-control, as children's needs must be met, regardless of the urgency of the mother's needs. Feeding the family, already her responsibility, becomes an easy arena for the expression of extreme needs for control. Mothers may personalize normal struggles with their children, struggles that reflect the child's developmental level as much as the mother's behaviors. For example, mothers may complain that "my three-year-old won't obey me anymore when I tell her to sit at the table to eat" or "I can never cook anything my teenagers like." Addressing these struggles and confusions early on can help a couple establish a more positive relationship and feel more comfortable in shared parenting activities.

Pregnancy: Excitement and Anxiety

Pregnancy is a time of enormous weight preoccupation in our culture. Obstetricians routinely mention weight in regular prenatal checkups, and most often castigate women for gaining more than is recommended. Well-meaning friends constantly ask, "When are you due?" then look you over, assessing whether your weight gain is appropriate for your due date. Thus, while women watch their bodies change, more aware than ever of their vulnerability to biological factors, their doctors and friends constantly monitor their weight, giving them little comfort or feelings of security in trusting their own bodies. Yet, during pregnancy, as at other times, weight gain is heavily biological. How much one gains—and how it is distributed on the body—varies widely from person to person. Well-trained obstetricians agree with mine, who wisely says, "We worry more about the underweight woman who gains little weight than about how many pounds most women gain during pregnancy."

Pregnancy dramatically illustrates our culture's ambivalence toward food. In many cultures, it is considered a compliment to be thought pregnant, whether one is or not. In our culture, the greatest *faux pas* is to guess that someone is pregnant and be wrong, for such an error implies that the other person has gained weight. When I was seven months pregnant, my mother repeatedly suggested I not stand with my hands folded around my stomach, because it emphasized how big I was.

The woman with a history of eating concerns is particularly vulnerable during pregnancy. Because body shape and weight gain are largely outside of one's control, and one's body is going through such tremendous and unfamiliar changes, eating concerns and related emotional issues (such as the mother-daughter relationship, self-control, and self-esteem) that have been addressed at earlier stages in one's life may reappear, making one feel particular panic and loss of control. On the other hand, some compulsive dieters may experiment with eating in healthful ways, for the first time in their lives allowing themselves to eat the foods they crave in the amounts they want. They may fear their loss of control, however, and their weight gain, not realizing that they can trust their body signals and approach healthier eating if they allow themselves to pay attention to body signals.

The conventional wisdom is that a pregnant woman is "eating for two." Although one does not need to double one's calorie intake, one does need to pay particular attention to healthful, balanced eating that provides maximum nutrients and avoids processed or high fat foods. Moderate exercise, particularly walking, should be continued throughout pregnancy.

Pregnancy can be an enormously freeing time for women. As body needs are changing, women find they experience unexpected cravings—perhaps for pickles, ice cream, garbanzo beans, trail mix, or (as I did) boiled eggs! Learning to listen to body needs can set the stage for better eating habits after the baby is born.

Mothering: Can It Make You Fat?

Childbearing changes a woman's body chemistry and her self-definition. Here is a new life to take care of—but here, too, are new challenges to deal with.

Breastfeeding intensifies the sense of responsibility for this new child and, for many women, is an intensely rewarding experience. Biologically, breastfeeding helps the mother's body to readjust to its prepregnancy state, and breastfeeding women are likely to lose weight sooner. Their children show greater resistance to illnesses. Further, breastfed babies gain weight more slowly and switch to solid foods later than bottlefed. Bottlefeeding may, however, be more convenient and reasonable for mothers who return to work early on or who struggle with feelings of incompetency at nurturing others.

Bottlefeeding and breastfeeding involve different parent-child dynamics, with breastfeeding encouraging greater interaction with the infant and awareness of her needs. Bottlefeeding, however, allows fathers to participate in feeding their babies. With bottlefeeding, it is easier to estimate how much the baby is getting. Although one may also underfeed breastfed infants, the tendency is greater to overfeed bottlefed infants, or to use external standards, rather than the baby's own satiety, as a measure of his or her fullness. To counteract these, bottlefed babies should always be held during feeding, and a baby should not be cajoled into finishing the bottle if she is rejecting the nipple.

Motherhood may be fattening. The biological changes accompanying pregnancy seem to predispose some women to weight gain, particularly after multiple pregnancies. A certain amount of fat is necessary for ovulation to take place, and for sustaining a pregnancy. These changes in adipose tissue may not reverse themselves after the pregnancy ends and women may find their set point has adjusted to a higher level, contributing to weight gain.

Menopause: Coming to Terms with Aging

Menopause disrupts established eating patterns, attitudes toward body and sexuality, and self-esteem. In our culture, menopause is considered painful and traumatic. Women are "punished" more than men for aging, and menopause symbolizes this transition. Our stereotypes at this time are all the negative stereotypes of femaleness: irritability, mood swings, and menstrual pain. These attitudes toward aging contribute to weight gain for many women. Women may try to assuage their fears about getting older and "losing" their femininity by eating more chaotically.

The physiological changes of middle adulthood make some weight gain inevitable and desirable. Many women's metabolism slows down with menopause, increasing their tendency to gain weight. Further, whether they have children or not, their activity level tends to slow down. Feelings of loss engendered by the empty nest may become more acute unless women actively establish new, independent goals and activities.

Later Adulthood: Good Eating Habits Pay Off in the Long Run

Elderly people, particularly elderly women, are often in surprisingly good health. Our assumption that old age is necessarily decrepit is a false assumption, as many of my older friends will quickly tell you.

Yet, elderly women are particularly vulnerable to eating problems. They are well aware of their changing physiology—muscle atrophy, medical complications, changes in body shape—and may feel increasingly isolated from friends and family. Cooking for others happens less frequently and older women may choose to simplify food preparation by heating up a can of beans or eating only one fast-food item. Many elderly women have been placed on diets by their doctors because of medical problems, further complicating their sense of self and their body image. Although these diets are sometimes helpful, they occur at a time when women may be struggling with reduced senses of taste and smell. For these reasons, elderly women, particularly if they are widowed or living alone, are particularly vulnerable to inadequate nutrition and caloric intake, exacerbating health problems. For good eating habits to continue, these women may need external support to help them continue to eat well-balanced, healthy meals.

At a recent meeting I led at the local Red Cross, the group of elderly women in attendance asked for help with doctor-imposed diets. Doctors are quick to hand out diets without considering that they are rarely effective. Although these women longed to weigh the same as when they married, some weight gain is desirable among older women. Further, when weight control becomes necessary, it should not be based on a restriction or dieting model. Attempts to modify weight gain are more effective if they consider the individual's lifestyle and preferences, and encourage choice. Calories should not be excessively restricted, and any efforts to limit intake should be paired with moderate exercise, in whatever form is most comfortable for the individual.

Eating Our Way Through Life

Having a family that eats well probably means that you eat well yourself. Eat to satisfy your hunger and to glorify God. Don't impose diets on your family members. Talk health and moderation, not fear of fat. If help is needed, consider it wholistically—that is, treatment for the inner self as well as the body. Sensitize yourself to the destructive societal attitudes about weight, and don't perpetuate those attitudes. Prevention of eating problems is a societal as well as family and individual responsibility.

Men and women, during their lifespan, have a tendency to gain weight. In addition to a biological propensity to gain weight with age, weight gain seems the result of poor eating habits and reduced exercise. For women, further, the stages of life often seem accompanied by physiological changes which encourage weight gain. Adhering to societal standards for thinness, particularly for older women struggling to be younger by being as thin as a younger woman, puts unrealistic pressures on women. By coming to terms with inevitable weight gain, and by learning to eat more wholistically and healthily, we enhance the distinctive pleasures of each stage of life.

10.

You Can Change How You Eat!

Hildy had been a restrictive eater and occasional vomiter for twenty years before she became pregnant. She worried that she would pass on her eating problems to her daughter, but she was unable to change her disordered patterns of eating, even through her pregnancy. However, at the birth of her daughter, Hildy was so moved by God's gift of a healthy baby that she was empowered to change. "One day at a time" was her motto as she struggled daily, even hourly to control her intake and output. Now, fifteen months after Harriet's birth, Hildy continues free of self-induced vomiting, and is able to eat foods that she claims she's never tasted before. She still has moments of fear of food, but she also has moments of joy in her eating.

Confronting ourselves is no easy task. Changing the way we do things is even tougher. But it *is* possible. In this book, we have emphasized the necessity of "renewing our minds" as integral to establishing a lifetime pattern of healthy eating. We have offered a framework for self-exploration, for honestly examining ourselves and thus building a foundation for lasting change. And lasting change happens when we face the facts, face our feelings, and face our false beliefs.

Face the Facts

The first step in changing involves learning all you can learn about the problem you are confronting. There are so many half-truths floating around about weight, eating problems, and health that it is difficult to sort out fact from fiction, difficult to know where to begin to solve one's own eating problems. In this book we have outlined a few basic principles and truths that are consistent with the best research on our physiological functioning and also mesh with basic biblical principles of spiritual health.

For instance, dieting is an ineffective way to feel happy with your body. Restrictive eating can be dangerous to your health and may contribute directly to outbursts of overeating. Binge eating, purging, starving oneself, taking chemicals, and vomiting all send your body into metabolic crisis that undercuts your efforts to care for yourself. Overeating and undereating are habits that have been learned by practice, and so can be unlearned with a little more practice. We must learn to tune in to our body, hearing its signals of hunger and restlessness. Then we must choose actions that will meet its needs, nurturing it gently with food and movement.

Face Your Feelings

As we discussed in our chapter on eating and emotional pain, we can numb ourselves with food. We can worry about calories rather than wondering if we are satisfied with our major life choices. We can fill our emptiness, our boredom, our neediness with junk food. We can express our anger by violent misuse of food and our bodies by starving, bingeing, and purging. We can validate our feelings of self-hatred by treating food in irresponsible and disgusting ways. We can victimize ourselves again and again, put ourselves at the mercy of food to mirror the ways we've been hurt in the past. We can master ultimate control by starving our bodies to prove that we are in control of ourselves. Yes, we can do all this, but in the doing we lose ourselves.

All of these emotional reasons behind wrong eating have developed as ways to cope with our pain. We are doing the best we can with what we've got. We are not bad or sick or self-indulgent. But at some point we can come to the realization that our wrong eating doesn't work for us anymore. It does not soothe our pain. Even when we diet we do not love ourselves. Even when we binge we can't forget our distress. Even when we purge we can't get rid of all the badness, the ugliness, the anger in our lives. Chaotic eating never solves any problem. When you realize that chaotic eating doesn't work for you, it is time to change. It is time to learn new ways to solve the problems that emotionally upset you. It is time to become self-nurturing and self-affirming, rather than self-punishing. It is time to learn the right way to eat—to eat in response to physical hunger, not emotional hunger.

Face Your False Beliefs

As Christians we are better able to examine our beliefs than most people. We know how to sort out the things that matter most. We know how to discern the right way, the way that brings us closer to being Christlike. Affirming ultimate values is not a new task for us, but we seldom apply those ultimate values to our eating. As we become more honest with ourselves, we can admit that our desperate need to be thin is motivated by the values of this world, not the values Christ would have us embody. When we give up connecting thinness with beauty, sexual attractiveness, positive self-esteem, and mature spirituality, we can take on more godly perspectives. Then we are free to choose and act in ways that meet our ultimate spiritual goals, rather than choosing and acting only in ways that enable us to stay on a diet. We can learn to be at home in our bodies, building up these temples of God in nourishing, satisfying ways.

The Uphill Struggle

Change does not happen overnight: Yesterday I was eating the wrong things for the wrong reasons; today I am healthy in every way. The actual process of doing things today differently from the way we did them yesterday is an uphill struggle. It is easy to put our own desires for change on a back burner as we concentrate on meeting others' needs. But we really don't have much to offer other people if we cannot affirm ourselves on a deep level.

Following through on change can be a boring, slow process. Keep your expectations reasonable. Avoid toxic words like *never*, *only*, and *forever*. Listen to any attempts to rationalize away your initial energy for change by giving yourself a variety of stalling, distracting messages:

> *This will be my last bag of potato chips so I might as well enjoy them all right now.*
>
> *Eating in response to physical hunger sounds like a ridiculous idea; maybe my doctor wouldn't approve of it.*
>
> *I feel in good control today so I'll skip a meal to balance out that splurge of last week.*
>
> *If I try to sit with my feelings right now, I'd probably explode and hurt someone, so it is safer to crunch along on these peanuts.*
>
> *Purging can't be that bad for you if you only do it now and again.*
>
> *I am not really anorexic; I am just a successful dieter.*
>
> *How can I be sensitive to hunger cues here at the church potluck? I want a taste of everything.*
>
> *I've just got to be as thin as the pastor's wife; she is such a model of good living for us.*
>
> *I know I can't trust my body . . . never could and never will.*

Do these excuses sound familiar? When you hear yourself saying things that don't make sense, acknowledge them rather than denying them. When you feel like you have a committee inside your head and all the members of the committee have a different opinion, hear out all the internal voices. Listen to their fears patiently, but vote for action with the voice that offers hope, encouragement, and a constructive plan.

When you know it is time for change, do it. Practice change at every opportunity. Don't put it off for a better day. Practice the principles of right eating consciously, directly, frequently. Check in with your hungers, both physical and emotional, several times an hour if necessary. Take the time to ask yourself what you need, what you want at this very moment. Comment to yourself that you feel good about yourself, about your body, at this moment when you are at work, at play, at rest. Identify and change things when you recognize that you are nervous, agitated, depressed, or in any conflict. As you put your energy into changing your behavior, choices, and attitudes, you will begin to pick up positive signs of progress—and be further motivated.

Why Can't It Happen Right Now?

Unless we make a daily commitment to lasting change, our efforts will be frustrated. The Bible offers us examples of miraculous change, most noticeably in the healing ministry of Jesus, but even these changes are maintained by disciplined follow-up. For instance, when Jesus healed Jairus's daughter he told her to rise and eat something to sustain her strength. The instantaneous healing was enabled by her choosing to eat and her family providing her nourishment.

Or consider the recurring metaphor of the kingdom of God as leaven or yeast that works its way through the loaf gradually but totally. The leaven works thoroughly from the inside out until the bread is wholesome and imbued with the spirit of health. However, after the bread has risen once it usually needs to be pressed down and kneaded to make the yeast mixed in even more thoroughly. This temporary setback only serves to make the leaven work more effectively.

Indeed, setbacks are *part* of the process, evidence that you are changing in a deep-down way. Be kind to yourself when you make mistakes. You may feel a strong resistance to trying out something new—as if parts of yourself that you didn't even know about are putting up barriers and blockades to change. We are complicated creatures and too often in conflict with ourselves, just as Paul commented that we do the things we do not want to do and don't do the things we want to do. This ambivalence sometimes inhibits constructive change. That is why change usually becomes real in little ways, a slow process of insight about what we should be doing at any given time.

We Can't Go It Alone!

It is almost impossible to change all by yourself. Christians don't make very good loners. We are designed to live in community; we are called to be members of the body of Christ. We are best at facing and solving our problems within the context of our community of faith.

In practical terms there are many ways to draw upon your community of faith for the resources to deal with a chaotic eating problem. Even from a distance we—the authors, the clients who taught us that these ideas work, and the other readers who will try these solutions—are in community with you as you face your eating difficulties. We are your silent cheering squad; we are fellow strugglers working at understanding and meeting our hungers.

Our faith communities will respond to the problem of wrong eating as we make our voices heard in expressing our need for support. Sometimes it takes a great deal of courage to raise this issue with a clear enough voice, a strong enough voice, so that our leaders can take our needs seriously. Some churches already sponsor discussion groups, reading groups, or groups specifically focused on weight loss. These groups, even though they may be misguided in their endorsement of dieting, offer a safe place to share your own struggles with food. Christian counseling centers are increasingly able to offer specialized groups for anorexics, bulimics, and chaotic eaters of all types because they have recognized the need to deal with eating problems. Working individually with a Christian therapist trained to deal with eating problems may sometimes be the easiest and most effective way to mobilize support and gain insight into your process of change.

It is most important to find a prayer partner, a confidante who is ready to listen and respond to the specifics of your eating problems. It may be helpful to find a woman who also has difficulties with food so that you can be a mutual resource for each other. Find someone who makes you feel comfortable and accepted, no matter what eating mistakes you may make in the process of change. With a prayer partner, honesty is more important than image. If you find yourself worrying about what she will think of you for doing one thing or another, confess it to God and to her as soon as you can. To deal with an eating problem, you must be doing it for yourself in the sight of God, not to meet someone else's approval.

Together work out a plan for implementing change in your lives. Regular times for talking and praying are just as important as her help during the eating crises, when you need to call her from the Chinese restaurant about your impulse to binge. Perhaps utilizing the "What Does the Bible Say?" exercise would give you a focus for Bible study to explore biblical foundations about eating. Or check in a concordance for the word *eat* and begin looking up and reading the hundreds of biblical references about eating and food. Share with her the everyday revelations and insights you gain from watching your children, participating in relationships, achieving at work, or sharing your talents in church. Listen to her struggles; let them resonate with your own until the interconnecting of thoughts, feelings, memories, hopes, ideas, and pain yields clarity, insight, and conviction.

At Home in Ourselves, at Home in God

God has promised to be with us in all that we do. That does not mean that things will always be easy. Even during the tough times, God calls us to discipline and accountability. Even when we fail, God loves us. When we are in good control of our eating, we can be humble. When we feel at home within ourselves we can feel truly at home in God. We can do all things through Christ who strengthens us. Since victory is assured, all we need to do is claim it with the daily walk of discipleship—the daily commitment to right eating.

The heavenly banquet, a Christian metaphor for ultimate union with God, will offer lots of good feasting. We won't be worried about our eating then. We won't be frantic about our body size. We won't be watching how much our neighbor overeats. We won't even think about leaving the table too full, or too hungry, or too angry. We will be filled and we will be enjoying it.

O God, our Creator, our Redeemer, our Sustainer, we praise you for creating us unique; we are wonderfully and fearfully made. Remind us of your care as we struggle to follow in your ways. Wrap us in your safety when we feel that our hungers will overwhelm us. Encourage our courage as we face our fear of food. Give us attentiveness as we listen and respond to our physical hunger. Give us insight as we try to solve our emotional needs and hurts in more effective ways. Help us to keep our eyes on your beauty reflected in us rather than on the fashions of this world. Thank you for loving us no matter what. In all that we do, may we bring honor and glory to you. Amen.

Agencies

aaba (American anorexia-bulimia association, inc.)
133 Cedar Lane
Teaneck NJ 07666
201-836-1800.

ABC (Anorexia Bulimia Care, Inc.)
Box 213
Lincoln Center MA 01773
617-259-9767.

National Association to Aid Fat Americans
P.O. Box 188620
Sacramento CA 95818
916-443-0303.

Anorexics, Bulimics Anonymous
National Service Office
P.O. Box 47573
Phoenix AZ 85068
602-861-3295.

ANAD (National Association of Anorexia Nervosa and
  Associated Disorders)
Box 7
Highland Park IL 60035
312-831-3438.

BANA (Bulimia and Anorexia Nervosa Association)
401 Sunset Avenue
University of Windsor
Ontario Canada.

National Anorexic Aid Society
5796 Karl Road
Columbus OH 43229
614-895-2009.

Notes

Chapter 1

1. Kaye V. Cook, Karen Reiley, Ruth Stallsmith, and Helen Bray-Garretson, "Eating Concerns on Two Christian and Two Nonsectarian College Campuses: A Measure of Sex and Campus Differences in Attitudes Toward Eating," *Adolescence* 26, no. 102 (Summer 1991): 273–86.
2. Ibid.

Chapter 2

1. This exercise is adapted from Susie Orbach, *Fat is a Feminist Issue* (New York: Berkley, 1982), 145.
2. Ruth Striegel-Moore and Judith Rodin, "The Influence of Psychological Variables in Obesity." In Kelly Brownell and John Foreyt, *Handbook of Eating Disorders: The Physiology, Psychology, and Treatment of Obesity, Anorexia, and Bulimia* (New York: Basic Books, 1986).
3. Albert Stunkard, *The Pain of Obesity* (Palo Alto: Bull Publishing, 1976).
4. Stanley Schachter, "Some Extraordinary Facts About Obese Humans and Rats," *American Psychologist* 26, (1971): 129–44.
5. Paul Sorlie, Tavia Gordon, and William Kannel, "Body Build and Mortality: The Framingham Study," *Journal of the American Medical Association* 243, (1980): 1828–31.
6. Ancel Keys, "Overweight, Obesity, Coronary Heart Disease and Mortality," *Nutrition Reviews*, 38 (1980): 297–307.
7. George Bray, "Effects of Obesity on Health and Happiness." In Kelly Brownell and John Foreyt, *Handbook of Eating Disorders: The Physiology, Psychology, and Treatment of Obesity, Anorexia, and Bulimia* (New York: Basic Books, 1986).
8. Susan Wooley and Orland Wooley, "Obesity and Women: A Closer Look at the Facts," *Women's Studies International Quarterly* 2 (1979): 69–79.
9. Andrea Dazzi and Johanna Dwyer, "Nutritional Analyses of Popular Weight Reduction Diets in Books and Magazines," *International Journal of Eating Disorders* 3 (1984): 61–79.
10. Patricia Nicholas and Johanna Dwyer, "Diets for Weight Reduction: Nutritional Considerations." In Kelly Brownell and John

Foreyt, *Handbook of Eating Disorders: The Physiology, Psychology, and Treatment of Obesity, Anorexia, and Bulimia* (New York: Basic Books, 1986).

11. Joan Cavanaugh, *More of Jesus, Less of Me* (Plainville, NJ: Logos Int., 1976).

Chapter 3

1. Harrison Pope, and James Hudson, *New Hope for Binge Eaters*, (New York: McGraw Hill, 1984), 37.

2. Marlene Boskind-Lodahl, "Cinderella's Step-Sisters: A Feminist Perspective on Anorexia and Bulimia," *Signs: Journal of Women in Culture and Society* 2 (1976): 342–56.

3. J. Wardle and H. Beinart, "Binge Eating: A Theoretical Review," *British Journal of Clinical Psychology* 20 (1981): 97–109.

4. David Garner, Wendi Rockert, Marion Olmsted, Craig Johnson, and Donald Coscina, "Psychoeducational Principles in the Treatment of Bulimia and Anorexia Nervosa." In David Garner and Paul Garfinkel, *Handbook of Psychotherapy for Anorexia Nervosa and Bulimia* (New York: Guilford Press, 1985), 513–72.

5. Craig Johnson, "Initial Consultation for Patients with Bulimia and Anorexia Nervosa." In David Garner and Paul Garfinkel, *Handbook of Psychotherapy for Anorexia Nervosa and Bulimia* (New York: Guilford Press, 1985), 19–54.

6. Susan Wooley and Orland Wooley, "Feeling Fat in a Thin Society," *Glamour* (February 1984): 198–201, 251–52.

7. Maria Root, Patricia Fallon, and William Friedrich, *Bulimia: A Systems Approach to Treatment* (New York: W. W. Norton, 1986).

Chapter 4

1. P. D. Slade and Gerald Russell, "Awareness of Body Dimension in Anorexia Nervosa: Cross-Sectional and Longitudinal Studies," *Psychological Medicine* 3, (1973): 188–99.

2. Cherry Boone O'Neill, *Starving for Attention* (New York: Continuum, 1982), 80–81.

3. Stephen Levenkron, *Kessa* (New York: Warner Books, 1986), 79–80.

4. Hilde Bruch, *The Golden Cage: The Enigma of Anorexia Nervosa* (Cambridge, Mass.: Harvard University Press, 1978), 23.

5. Salvador Minuchin, Bernice Rosman, and Lester Baker, *Psychosomatic Families: Anorexia Nervosa in Context* (Cambridge, Mass.: Harvard University Press, 1978).

6. Stephen Levenkron, *Kessa* (New York: Warner Books, 1986), 7.
7. David Garner and Kelly Bemis, "Cognitive Therapy for Anorexia Nervosa." In David Garner and Paul Garfinkel, *Handbook of Psychotherapy for Anorexia Nervosa and Bulimia* (New York: Guilford Press, 1985), 107–46.

Chapter 5
1. Judith Rodin, Lisa Silberstein, and Ruth Striegel-Moore, "Women and Weight: A Normative Discontent." In T. B. Sonderegger, ed., *Nebraska Symposium on Motivation, 1984: Psychology and Gender* (Lincoln: University of Nebraska Press, 1985).
2. Janet Polivy and C. Peter Herman, "Dieting and Binging," *American Psychologist* 40 (1985), 193–210.
3. Ibid.
4. Richard Keesey, "A Set Point Analysis of the Regulation of Body Weight." In Albert J. Stunkard, ed., *Obesity* (Philadelphia: W. B. Saunders, 1980).
5. Geneen Roth, *Breaking Free from Compulsive Eating* (Indianapolis: Bobbs-Merrill, 1984).
6. Jane Brody, *Good Food Book: Living the High Carbohydrate Way* (New York: Norton, 1985).

Chapter 6
1. Susie Orbach, *Fat Is a Feminist Issue II: A Program to Conquer Compusive Eating* (New York: Berkley Books, 1982).
2. Kaye V. Cook and Lance Lee, *Man and Woman, Alone and Together: Gender Roles, Identity and Intimacy in a Changing Culture* (Wheaton, Ill: Victor Press, 1992).
3. Harriet Lerner, *Dance of Anger* (New York: Harper & Row, 1985).
4. Maria Root, Patricia Fallon, and William Friedrich, *Bulimia: A Systems Approach to Treatment* (New York: Norton, 1986).
5. David Finkelhor, *Sexually Victimized Children* (New York: Free Press, 1979).
6. Ellen Bass and Laura Davis, *The Courage to Heal: A Guide for Women Survivors of Child Sexual Abuse* (New York: Harper & Row, 1988).
7. Anne Wilson Schaef, *Codependence: Misunderstood—Mistreated* (San Francisco: Harper & Row, 1986).
8. Stephanie Covington and Liana Beckett, *Leaving the Enchanted Forest* (San Francisco: Harper & Row, 1988).

Chapter 7

1. Christopher Fairburn, "Cognitive-Behavioral Treatment for Bulimia." In David Garner and Paul Garfinkel, *Handbook of Psychotherapy for Anorexia Nervosa and Bulimia* (New York: Guilford Press, 1985).
2. David Garner, Wendi Rochert, Marion Olmsted, Craig Johnson, and Donald Coscina, "Psychoeducational Principles in the Treatment of Bulimia and Anorexia Nervosa." In David Garner and Paul Garfinkel, *Handbook of Psychotherapy for Anorexia Nervosa and Bulimia* (New York: Guilford Press, 1985), 517.
3. April Fallon and Paul Rozin, "Sex Differences in Perception of Desirable Body Shape," *Journal of Abnormal Psychology* 94 (1985): 102–105.
4. Hilde Bruch, *Eating Disorders* (New York: Basic Books, 1973), 189.

Chapter 8

1. Doris Longacre, *More-with-Less Cookbook* (Scottsdale, Penn., 1976).
2. Evelyn Birge Vitz, *A Continual Feast* (New York: Harper & Row, 1985).

Chapter 9

1. Steven Gortmaker, William Dietz, and A. M. Sobel, "Increasing Pediatric Obesity in the U.S." *American Journal of Diseases of Children* 141 (May 1987): 535–40.
2. Ellyn Satter, *How to Get Your Kid to Eat . . . But Not Too Much* (Palo Alto, Calif.: Bull Publishing, 1987).
3. Kaye V. Cook, Karen Reiley, Ruth Stallsmith, and Helen Bray-Garretson, "Eating Concerns on Two Christian and Two Nonsectarian College Campuses: A Measure of Sex and Campus Differences in Attitudes Toward Eating," *Adolescence* 26 (Summer 1991): 273–86

Resources for Further Reading

Bankson, Marjory. *Braided Streams: Esther and a Woman's Way of Growing*. San Diego: Luramedia, 1985.

Bass, Ellen, and Laura Davis. *The Courage to Heal: A Guide for Women Survivors of Child Sexual Abuse*. New York: Harper & Row, 1988.

Bennett, William, and Joel Gurin. *The Dieter's Dilemma*. New York: Basic Books, 1982.

Boskind-White, Marlene, and William White. *Bulimarexia: The Binge-Purge Cycle*. New York: Norton, 1983.

Bruch, Hilde. *Eating Disorders*. New York: Basic Books, 1973.

_____. *The Golden Cage: The Enigma of Anorexia Nervosa*. Cambridge: Harvard University Press, 1978.

Brynteson, Paul. *Fitness and Faith*. Nashville: Thomas Nelson, 1985.

Cauwels, Janice. *Bulimia: The Binge-Purge Compulsion*. New York: Doubleday, 1983.

Chernin, Kim. *The Hungry Self: Women, Eating, and Identity*. New York: Harper & Row, 1985.

_____. *The Obsession: Reflections on the Tyranny of Slenderness*. New York: Harper & Row, 1981.

Clark, Mary Franzen. *Hiding, Hurting, Healing*. Grand Rapids, Mich.: Zondervan, 1985.

Freedman, Rita. *Bodylove: Learning to Like Our Looks—And Ourselves*. Carlsbad, Calif.: Gurze Books, 1986.

Garner, David, and Paul Garfinkel. *Handbook of Psychotherapy for Anorexia Nervosa and Bulimia*. New York: Guilford Press, 1985.

Hall, Lindsey, and Leigh Cohn. *Bulimia: A Guide to Recovery*. Carlsbad, Calif.: Gurze Books, 1986.

_____. *Self-Esteem: Tools for Recovery*. Carlsbad, Calif.: Gurze Books, 1990.

Hutchinson, Marcia. *Transforming Body Image: Learning to Love the Body You Have*. Carlsbad, Calif.: Gurze Books, 1985.

Kano, Susan. *Making Peace with Food: Freeing Yourself from the Diet/Weight Obsession*. New York: Harper & Row, 1989.

Lerner, Harriet. *The Dance of Intimacy*. New York: Harper & Row, 1989.

_____. *The Dance of Anger: A Woman's Guide to Changing the Patterns of Intimate Relationships*. New York: Harper & Row, 1985.

Miller, Caroline Adams. *Feeding the Soul: Daily Meditations for Recovering from Eating Disorders*. New York: Bantam Books, 1991.

O'Neill, Cherry Boone. *Starving for Attention*. New York: Continuum, 1982.

Orbach, Susie. *Fat Is a Feminist Issue II: A Program to Conquer Compulsive Eating*. New York: Berkley, 1982.

Palmer, R. L. *Anorexia Nervosa: A Guide for Sufferers and Their Families*. England: Penguin Books, 1980.

Polivy, Janet, and C. Peter Herman. *Breaking the Diet Habit: The Natural Weight Alternative*. New York: Basic Books, 1983.

Roberts, Nancy. *Breaking All the Rules: Feeling Good and Looking Great, No Matter What Your Size*. New York: Pengrove, 1987.

Roth, Geneen. *Why Weight? A Guide to Ending Compulsive Eating*. New York: New American, 1989.

_____. *Breaking Free from Compulsive Eating*. Indianapolis: Bobbs-Merrill, 1984.

Roth, Geenen. *Feeding the Hungry Heart*. New York: Signet, 1982.

Rowland, Cynthia. *The Monster Within: Overcoming Bulimia*. Grand Rapids, Mich.: Baker, 1984.

Sanford, Linda, and Mary Ellen Donovan. *Women and Self-Esteem: Understanding and Improving the Way We Think and Feel About Ourselves*. New York: Penguin, 1984.

Satter, Ellyn. *How to Get Your Kid to Eat . . . But Not Too Much*. Palo Alto, Calif.: Bull Publishing, 1987.

_____. *Child of Mine: Feeding with Love and Good Sense*. Palo Alto, Calif.: Bull Publishing, 1983.

Siegel, M., J. Brisman, and M. Weinshel. *Surviving an Eating Disorder: Strategies for Family and Friends*. New York: Harper & Row, 1988.

Stuart, Mary, and Lynnzy Orr. *Otherwise Perfect: People and Their Problems with Weight*. Pompano Beach, Fla.: Health Communications, 1987.

Surrey, Janet. *Eating Patterns as a Reflection of Women's Development*. Work in Progress Series, Stone Center, Wellesley College, 1984.

Vredevelt, Pam, and Joyce Whitman. *Walking a Thin Line: Anorexia and Bulimia, the Battle Can Be Won*. Portland, Ore.: Multnomah Press, 1985.

Woititz, Janet. *Struggle for Intimacy*. Pompano Beach, Fla.: Health Communications, 1985.

Wooley, Susan, and Orland Wooley. Eating Disorders: Obesity and Anorexia. In Brodsky, Annette, and Rachel Hare-Mustin, *Women and Psychotherapy*. New York: Guilford, 1980.

THE **LIFELINES FOR RECOVERY** SERIES

Zondervan's **Lifelines for Recovery** series emphasizes healthy, step-by-step approaches for dealing with specific critical issues.